signature styles

signature styles

20 Stitchers Craft Their Look

Jenny Doh

LARK
CRAFTS

An Imprint of Sterling Publishing Co., Inc.
New York

WRITER & CHIEF EDITOR
Jenny Doh

WRITER & COPY EDITOR
Amanda Crabtree

ASSISTANT EDITORS
Cynthia Shaffer
Jana Holstein
Sarah Meehan
Monica Mouet

COVER DESIGNER
Kristi Pfeffer

DESIGNER
Raquel Joya

Library of Congress Cataloging-in-Publication Data

Doh, Jenny.
 Signature styles : 20 stitchers craft their look / Jenny Doh. -- 1st ed.
   p. cm.
 Includes index.
 ISBN 978-1-60059-791-6 (pb - flexibound : alk. paper)
 1. Dressmaking. 2. Sewing. I. Title.
 TT515.D63 2011
 646.4'04--dc22

                              2010040531

10 9 8 7 6 5 4 3 2 1

First Edition

Published by Lark Crafts
An Imprint of Sterling Publishing Co., Inc.
387 Park Avenue South, New York, NY 10016

Text © 2011, Jenny Doh
Photography © 2011, Lark Crafts, an Imprint of Sterling Publishing Co., Inc.,
unless otherwise specified
Illustrations © 2011, Lark Crafts, an Imprint of Sterling Publishing Co., Inc.,
unless otherwise specified

Distributed in Canada by Sterling Publishing,
c/o Canadian Manda Group, 165 Dufferin Street
Toronto, Ontario, Canada M6K 3H6

Distributed in the United Kingdom by GMC Distribution Services,
Castle Place, 166 High Street, Lewes, East Sussex, England BN7 1XU

Distributed in Australia by Capricorn Link (Australia) Pty Ltd.,
P.O. Box 704, Windsor, NSW 2756 Australia

If you have questions or comments about this book, please contact:
Lark Crafts
67 Broadway
Asheville, NC 28801
828-253-0467

Manufactured in China

ISBN 13: 978-1-60059-791-6

For information about custom editions, special sales, premium and corporate
purchases, please contact Sterling Special Sales Department at 800-805-5489 or
specialsales@sterlingpub.com.

For information about desk and examination copies available to college and
university professors, requests must be submitted to academic@larkbooks.com.
Our complete policy can be found at www.larkcrafts.com.

INTRODUCTION

What I wear and how I present myself speak volumes. This is why I love to incorporate handmade, one-of-a-kind items into my attire, and to layer all components in unique and unexpected ways. By doing so, I know I am communicating my confidence, my imagination, and my creativity to the world. When I'm able to compose outfits that are spot-on, I love how I don't really even need to utter a word in order to command the attention of an entire roomful of people.

From childhood to adolescence to womanhood, I've experimented with lots of different types of clothing, and in the process, developed the essence of my signature style. But the great thing about style is that it continually evolves, as we all remain open to studying the modes of others.

Those who influence me the most don't necessarily have Hollywood star status. For example, it's the woman in the grocery store who drapes a beautiful scarf over her trench coat. It's the guy at the gym whose T-shirt is oh-so-wonderfully tattered and distressed. It's a colleague who pairs a totally hot pair of stilettos with a classic black dress. In short, when I see people who care enough to make an impression, it impresses me.

It is also the courageously innovative and hard-working women within the creative community who provide me with endless inspiration...the kind of women who have gathered within the pages of *Signature Styles* and who welcome you into their homes, their studios, and their closets.

They are: **Heather Bailey**, **Serena Thompson**, **Meg McElwee**, **Elsie Flannigan**, **Rashida Coleman-Hale**, **Kathy Cano-Murillo**, **Betz White**, **Meg Allan Cole**, **Bari J. Ackerman**, **Erika & Monika Simmons**, **Kayte Terry**, **Megan Hunt**, **Sonya Nimri**, **Megan Nicolay**, **Ruth Singer**, **Sandy Stone**, **Bonzie & Ger**, **Teva Durham**, and **Amy Tangerine**.

As you read their intriguing profiles, you will learn the unique journey that each of them has traveled to develop their points of view. The added bonus to learning their inspired stories is also learning firsthand how to create a distinctive piece of clothing or accessory that they have designed just for you. Because every one of you has your own distinct style, feel free to use these projects as creative springboards, adjusting fabrics, colors, and embellishments to suit *your* signature style.

I dedicate this book to my beloved Gerardo, Monica, and Andrew—the best "accessories" a woman could ever have. On behalf of the entire *Signature Styles* team, I thank you for joining us and welcome you to an experience that will undoubtedly be unforgettable.

With style,

Jenny Doh

www.crescendoh.com

7

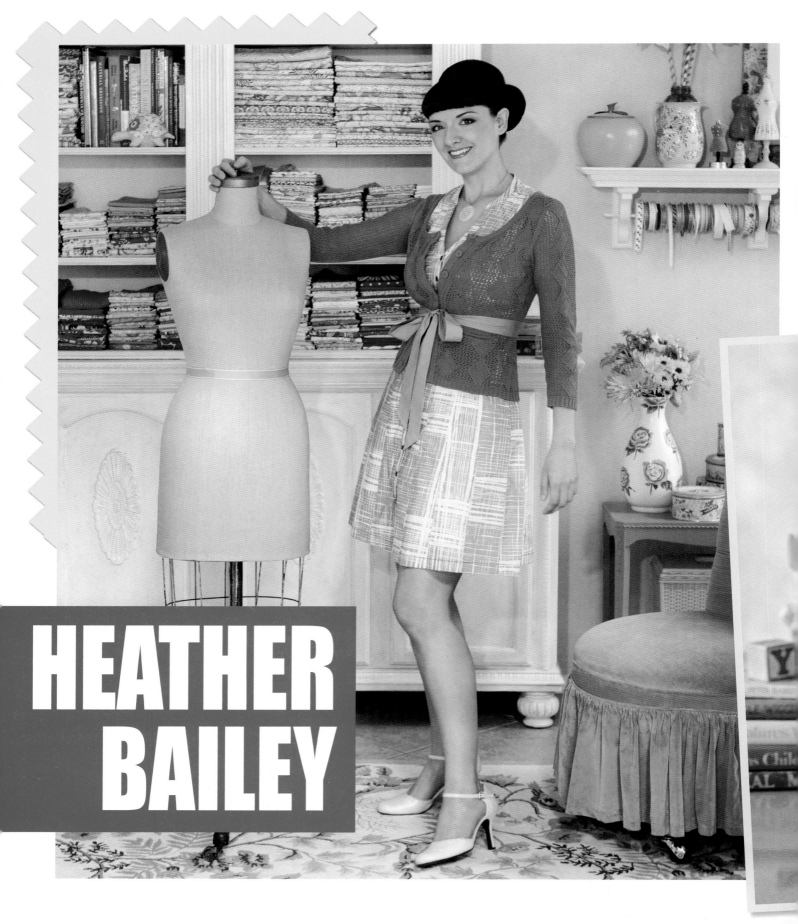

HEATHER BAILEY

www.heatherbailey.typepad.com
www.heatherbaileystore.com

Heather Bailey is known for her fresh and colorful fabric designs, papercraft products, and sewing patterns. She spreads happiness with everything she creates, while building a business she is passionate about. Heather also writes and photographs for her blog, which details her crafting projects and life with her husband and two kids.

FROM AN AHA MOMENT TO CREATIVITY

Heather originally planned on becoming a surgeon. She skipped her senior year of high school to go to college on scholarship early. Every semester she took one creative class just for fun and stress relief. When she eventually realized it would be hard to be both a surgeon and a mom—something that was, and still is, very important to her—she decided to further explore classes that would broaden her creative horizons. Once she focused seriously on clothing design, she had an aha moment. She realized that what truly brought her joy could also be her career.

Heather had her son right out of college. Her husband's first job was in Hollywood, where they lived on a tight budget. With one car between them, she often spent entire days with her son in a tiny apartment. Heather knew she had to do something to change their financial situation. "I didn't have any resources, but that high-pressure situation gave me a lot of skills. I had to learn how to be resourceful—I came to understand why the caged bird sings." With determination Heather learned to sing by flying toward her true calling. "That's when I found my own love of happiness, happy clothing, and happy artwork," she says.

9

No matter how busy life gets, it is very important to Heather to find ways to prioritize quality time with her family.

Because of those experiences, she created a company centered on showcasing joy. She likes to think of herself as a designer of all things happy. "Happy projects for a beautiful life—for me, that's my song," says Heather. By creating beauty in hard circumstances, she developed the confidence to create without hesitation, and eventually won the financial freedom her family needed.

HOBBIES & HAPPINESS

Heather is definitely a night person. "It's when I feel I'm on creative fire," she says. "I'm trying to harness that creative energy during the day, so I can also manage my business." When she's not working, Heather enjoys exploring new creative avenues. "My favorite hobby is learning new things," she says. "My hobby is collecting hobbies." Over the years, she has gained skills in mediums ranging from stained glass to lampwork beads to knitwear. One thing she wants to do is oil paint, particularly figure painting. "If you can fit the human body, you can fit anything," she says. "I feel painting is the same way. If you can paint the human body, you can paint anything."

Heather's inspiration comes from the happy items she displays in her studio. She has several vintage toys and dolls perched on shelves and cabinets. "They make me happy," says Heather, "and that's all that matters. If an item passes the happiness test, it's justified to be in my studio." She also loves having her supplies visible. "They encourage and inspire me," she says. She also loves to display anything her kids have made, whether it's one of her daughter's drawings or the Mother's Day tissue flower from her son. "Any time my kids make me something it's on my inspiration board," she says.

①

②

③

THE ESSENCE OF HEATHER'S STYLE

- Flowers in her hair

- Bright colors

- Something silly: "Whether it's a funny necklace or a flourish here or there, I like to wear something a little bit sassy that maybe your average person wouldn't have the nerve to wear."

- Antique jewelry, from antique stores or eBay: "I usually pick one piece to wear each day, whether it's a brooch or a necklace or something else."

- Fun shoes are the "easiest way to wake up an outfit."

① Heather loves to infuse bright colors not only into her fabrics and designs but also into her living space—like this fabulous chandelier. **②** Antique jewelry pieces like this one help Heather add focus and interest to her outfits. **③** Stacks of colorful fabric are omnipresent in Heather's studio.

11

2

1

HEATHER'S PRIZED WEARABLES

- A vintage fabric flower collection is her favorite way to turn an outfit into a palette: "I might be wearing a cream shirt and a yellow sweater but if I add a green flower to my hair, it's automatically an interesting palette."
- Red and cream striped sweater
- Great purses, from a beaded vintage purse to a cream purse with green and yellow flowers
- Embroidered peasant tops: "I hand stitch details on them, and I love how they can be dressed up or down."

1 Fresh flowers in bright and happy colors are frequently found in Heather's home and studio. **2** Sometimes, when an outfit is lacking in one color to complete a color palette, Heather pulls it all together by adorning her hair with the perfect flower.

FEARLESSNESS IN PERSONAL STYLE

Heather believes fashion is an established trend with popular appeal, whereas style comes from a creator. However, she doesn't think fashion and style are mutually exclusive: "You can have self-confidence in your own personal style while embracing both." For Heather, personal style comes from knowing yourself, having confidence in yourself, and knowing what you like. "Fashion comes into play when you are communicating your style so others can relate to you," she says.

Heather has always been confident when it comes to personal style. She has never been afraid to experiment, and claims, "A little bit of fearlessness is important." She began her exploration into personal style in the seventh grade, when she invented new hairstyles and hair accessories to go with them. She also remembers cutting the legs off overalls to make them into skirts. "I shortened things, added details," says Heather. "I was always playing."

Today, whether it's playing with her wardrobe or her newest fabric designs, Heather is always looking for an opportunity to spread happiness.

Heather enjoys collecting vintage handbags and unique new handbag designs that help complement the rest of her wardrobe.

13

This wristlet purse is the **perfect accessory** to complete many outfits—a piece that sings Heather's **signature tune** of **happy**.

HAPPY WRISTLET PURSE

WHAT YOU'LL NEED

Main fabric: ½-yard (45.7 cm)

Medium-weight, iron-on interfacing: ½ yard (45.7 cm)

Fleece interfacing: 13 x 13 inches (33 x 33 cm)

Lining fabric : 13 x 13 inches (33 x 33 cm)

Extra-heavy-weight interfacing: 11⅞ x 11⅞ inches (30.2 x 30.2 cm)

Thread in coordinating color

Rectangular metal ring: 1-inch (2.5 cm)

Zipper: 12-inch (30.5 cm)

Seam Allowance: ½-inch (1.3 cm), unless noted otherwise

1 Fold & Edge-Stitch the Handle

Cut the main fabric and medium-weight interfacing to each measure 14¾ x 3 inches (37.5 x 7.6 cm). Fuse the medium-weight interfacing to the wrong side of fabric. Fold in half and press. Fold raw edges into the center, forming a ¾-inch-wide (1.9 cm) strip, and press. Edge-stitch along each long side. Cut into two pieces: one 13 inches (33 cm) long and the other 1¾ inches (4.4 cm) long.

2 Attach Handle to Metal Ring

Slide the metal ring onto the 13-inch (33 cm) handle piece. With right sides together, fold handle in half and stitch ¼ inch (.6 cm) from raw edges. With the seam at the inside of the looped handle, slide the metal ring down close to the seam, then topstitch through the handle, ½ inch (1.3 cm) from earlier seam, to enclose metal ring and seam allowances. Fold shorter piece in half over the other side of metal ring. Stitch and set aside.

3 Layer Purse Fabrics

Cut the main fabric, medium-weight and fleece interfacing, and lining fabric each to measure 13 x 13 inches (33 x 33 cm). Cut extra-heavy-weight interfacing to measure 11⅞ x 11⅞ inches (30.2 x 30.2 cm). Center extra-heavy-weight interfacing (stiffener) on fleece interfacing and zigzag stitch around edge. Fuse interfacing to wrong side of main fabric. Center fleece on wrong side of interfaced fabric, with fleece side next to interfaced side of fabric and with stiffener side on top.

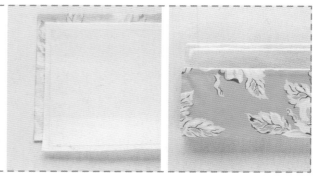

4 Attach the Zipper

With right sides together, position the zipper at the top front of the purse, with the zipper stop at your right. Sew the zipper to top of the purse. With right sides together, sew the other side of the zipper to the top back of purse (purse will make a cylinder shape).

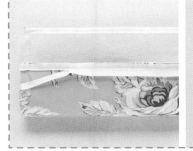

5 Attach the Handle

Position the handle on the left side of the purse front, ⅛ inch (.3 cm) below the zipper seam. Stitch to secure.

6 Attach the Lining

With right sides together, sew the lining to the top front of the purse along the zipper attachment seam. Repeat with other side of lining and top back of the purse.

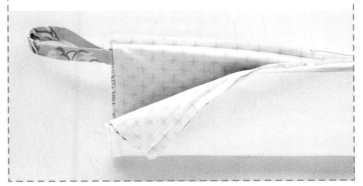

7 Stitch Sides of Purse

Stitch each side seam of the purse from the zipper down to the base of the purse. Repeat with lining side seams, leaving a 4-inch (10.1 cm) opening at one side of purse lining. Make a short ½-inch (1.3 cm) seam near zipper, and a longer 1½-inch (3.8 cm) seam at bottom.

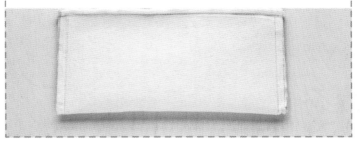

8 Form the Bottom Corners

Refold the bottom corners of the purse. From fold to fold, mark a 2-inch (5 cm) line perpendicular to each side seam. Stitch along the marked lines to form each bottom corner. Back-stitch at beginning and end of each seam. Press. Repeat with the bottom corners of lining.

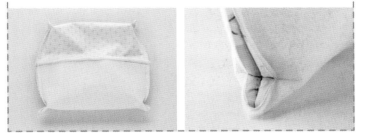

9 Turn, Press & Close

Turn the purse right side out through the opening. It may be necessary to roll the purse tightly to fit through the opening. Slipstitch the opening closed. Lightly press lining to inside of purse at zipper. Press as needed. Embellish by adding a fun zipper pull or splashy flower.

15

SERENA THOMPSON

Serena Thompson, who runs The Farm Chicks, a lifestyle brand and product line, has been in love with the feeling and style of the country since she was a little girl. Now, she shares that love through her blog, in the books she has written—including *The Farm Chicks in the Kitchen* and *The Farm Chicks Christmas*—and in her work as a consulting editor for *Country Living* magazine. Serena does all this while living with her husband and four boys in her dream location, the Northwestern United States.

HER PERSONAL TAKE ON STYLE

In her personal wardrobe, Serena loves to embrace trends while maintaining a style that speaks to her. "For me, fashion is what happens to be trendy at the moment, and style is my personal take on what I do with that fashion." Serena feels that she's always had style, being particularly influenced by members of her family from a young age. "My mom always had beautiful, effortless style," says Serena. "She looked beautiful without even trying." Her sister would order *Esprit* catalogs, and together they'd pore over the pages. "When we'd visit the city, we'd gape at every window display we could find, and leave feeling completely inspired."

As a child, Serena loved wearing hats, especially a beautiful old brown velvet beret that had once belonged to her grandma. Today, her style is also reflected in her home. "I love old signs and beautiful girly objects," says Serena. "The juxtaposition of the two is wonderful—junky and beautiful together is impactful."

TIME FOR FAMILY

Serena's day starts with getting her four boys ready for school. After they're off, she works out and then spends all day working on emails and business items and projects, mixed with laundry and cleaning. "Once the boys get out of school, we work on homework, get ready for dinner, and there's usually baseball games or track practice that follow," says Serena. "It's a blessing to be able to work from home."

THE ESSENCE OF SERENA'S STYLE

- Comfort
- Clothes that feel right: "I never wear something that needs to be constantly fluffed or moved around. What's the saying? 'Wear your clothes … don't let them wear you.'"
- Bright, happy colors
- Simple layering: the occasional sweater over shirt, or apron over jeans and a button-up
- T-shirts: "One of my favorite things to wear."

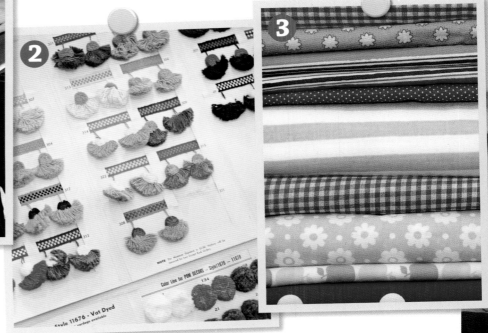

1 Shown with Serena is Amanda Panagos, who works closely with Serena at The Farm Chicks. **2** Serena lays out color swatches against a white background to determine which she likes the best. **3** Bright, cheery colors, like the blues and reds shown here, are among her favorite hues.

It's an exciting and busy time for Serena. She's opening a new store, working on magazine articles, publishing her daily blog, organizing her upcoming antiques show, designing a line of kitchenware, working on an anticipated retail project, and designing and building a new home—all while raising her boys. "It's a challenge," she says. "My husband, Colin, and I have always been big on setting priorities in our lives and staying true to them." Serena maintains a regimented day without much downtime. "I've become very choosy about what projects I agree to," she says. After all, her family is the one thing she couldn't live without. "I love what I have,"

Serena's favorite color palette includes a lot of white. Mixed with light pinks and reds, the colors radiate lightness and airiness.

she says, "but if I lost it all tomorrow, as long as I had my family, I'd be happy as a clam." She also credits her husband and marriage for helping her become who she is today. "He's a wonderful man who encourages me and has always believed in me. Without his support and faith, I'd never be where I am today, which is happy, content, and doing what I love."

Serena's attitude toward her family is one she hopes she exudes through her work as a Farm Chick. Even though many of her supporters and readers may not actually live in the country or have an actual farm, she believes the attitude of a Farm Chick is that of a happy home and a happy life wherever you live. Serena's favorite times are when she's at home relaxing with her family and friends. "A barbeque, an afternoon at the lake, something like that, and going to yard sales with my boys."

QUIET & EVOLVING INSPIRATION

Serena is most inspired by quiet moments. "I need time to hear nothing but silence, and to have a clear head," she says. "I think it comes from having a very quiet life as a child, living remotely and free of television." She spent the first years of her life in a hippie gypsy wagon, hand built by her father, wandering the back roads of the U.S., Canada, and Mexico.

1 Serena's sewing skills have evolved from her first days on a treadle sewing machine to her current sewing machine, where she spends time creating every day. **2** Serena loves the juxtaposition of an antique scale mixed with her new ribbons and rickrack. **3** The light orange of the books against the clean white shelves is a pleasing spot for Serena.

PEOPLE SERENA LOOKS TO FOR STYLE

- Her mom: "She was always draped in turquoise and Bohemian scarves long before they were cool."

- Her friend Celeste: "I love her collection of vintage clothing, and the way she mixes vintage with modern day. Celeste is stunning."

- Coco Chanel, Jackie O, and Audrey Hepburn: "All three of these women have an amazing classic, timeless style."

Serena's family eventually settled into a tiny cabin in the woods. She spent her days teaching herself to sew on a treadle sewing machine and to bake in a wood-burning stove because they didn't have running water, refrigeration, or electricity. Her family lived frugally, to which she credits her own thriftiness. She learned how to turn ordinary objects into something useful, and her creativity grew as a result.

When Serena lacks inspiration, she's learned that she can't force it. "I won't do it," she says. "If I just take my time, the inspiration comes to me. I've learned to be patient." She also makes a point to surround herself with her favorite colors for inspiration. "Every five or so years my favorite color palette seems to change as I evolve," says Serena, "but right now I'm loving lots of white. It's peaceful and serene to me." Bright and cheery colors, like pink and red, are also some of her favorites. Surrounding herself with inspiration helps Serena reach her goal of exuding style in what she creates and wears, and ultimately her goal of having a happy life.

SERENA'S PRIZED WEARABLES

- T-shirts
- Heels: "I wear them whenever possible."
- Her wedding pearls
- Pretty evening clutches: "I have a whole collection of them."
- Rhinestones
- Jeans

The jar of sprinkles reflects one of Serena's favorite relaxing activities: baking. Adding them to a jar is a fun way to show off the colors of both the sprinkles and the bright permanent markers.

SERENA'S SWEET-BUTTONED APRON

With this project Serena serves one up in her signature style—a **simple silhouette** that gets beautifully **enhanced** with the **cutest little touches**.

WHAT YOU'LL NEED

Template (page 141)

Red fabric: 1 yard (91.4 cm)

Red bias tape: 40 inches (102 cm) of ¼-inch width (.6 cm); 85 inches (216 cm) of ½-inch (1.3 cm) width

White fabric strips (2): 2 x 18 inches (5 x 45 cm)

Thread in coordinating color & hand needle

Red grosgrain ribbon, 1½ inches (3.8 cm) wide: 106 inches (269.2 cm)

Fabric-covered buttons: assorted colors & sizes

Seam Allowance: ½-inch (1.3 cm)

1 Cut Fabric & Stitch Bias Tape

Use the template on page 141 to cut the bodice portion of apron from red fabric. Also cut the skirt portion from same fabric to measure 36 x 24 inches (91.4 x 97 cm). Fold, pin, and stitch ¼-inch (.6 cm) red bias tape along the edges of the bodice. Fold, pin, and stitch ½-inch (1.3 cm) red bias tape along the edges of the skirt.

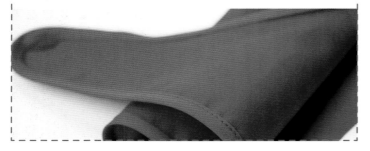

2 Gather & Pin

Add two running stitches at the top of the skirt and pull the threads to gather. For the waistband, cut light fabric to make two pieces that measure 2 x 18 inches (5 x 45.7 cm).

3 Attach the Waistband

Pin one of the strips to the skirt that has been gathered, with right sides together.

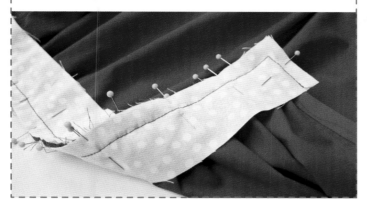

4 Turn the Waistband

Once everything is stitched, turn the waistband right side out.

5 Attach the Bodice

With right sides together pin and stitch the bodice to the center of one side of the waistband. (You are working on the right side of the apron.)

6 Topstitch

Pin everything together and add topstitching to the entire waistband area.

7 Create the Grosgrain Ties

Cut two pieces of 1½-inch-wide (3.8 cm) grosgrain ribbon, each measuring 30 inches (76.2 cm) long. Stitch these at the waist. Cut two pieces of 1½-inch-wide (3.8 cm) grosgrain ribbon that each measures 23 inches (58.4 cm). Stitch these onto the top for the neck tie.

8 Add Bright & Fun Buttons

Gather fabric-covered buttons in assorted sizes and attach to the neckline and waistline.

MEG McELWEE

www.sewliberated.com

Meg McElwee has helped pave the way for the modern sewer in her work as a pattern designer and artist. With her fun and fresh patterns and ideas, presented on both her website (above) and in her book of the same name, Meg makes sewing approachable and fun. Meg's talents carry over into her home life, where her style of simplicity and color and her love of family are both inspirational and a joy to witness.

A ROUTINE THAT WORKS

Because Meg works from home, her daily schedule can be flexible. But now that her son, Finn, is getting older, she's working on incorporating more routine into his day. "Before he was born, we could kind of go with the flow," says Meg. "We're still in the process of figuring out how to make more of a routine." Meg's husband, Patrick, helps run the Sew Liberated business from their home, where they divide up tasks in order to get it all done.

Meg takes Finn for the morning. They visit the science museum, run errands, ride bikes, create art, bake bread, or do a myriad of other activities. Then they join Patrick and the three of them eat lunch together; it's their big meal of the day. After that, Patrick takes Finn, and Meg gets to work. She only has about four hours each day to devote to her business. "This short amount of time is both liberating and difficult. I am constantly trying to efficiently shorten my to-do list." In order to do this, Meg has learned to say no. She also has had to lower expectations of how much she's able to do every day, whether it's keeping up her blog—including taking the photos and writing—designing, working on new patterns, or sewing.

When she has time to do whatever she likes, Meg enjoys being outside, and family music time. Both she and her husband play the guitar, and her husband plays the piano. "I sing, and Finn dances and sings right along with me. I love it," she says.

25

1 This branch is one of Meg's favorite pieces in her home. It holds 10 little perching birds of fabric and is suspended with fishing line so it looks like it's floating. **2** Meg's fabrics are organized by color in her studio for quick access when she's feeling inspired. **3** Meg is shown here wearing one of her favorite outfits—a T-shirt, jeans, and flat-soled boots.

THE ESSENCE OF MEG'S STYLE

- Well-fitting T-shirts, especially lower cut scoop neck or V-neck shirts

- A nice pair of good-fitting jeans: "They are worth the investment."

- Minimal accessories: "I don't wear earrings or a lot of jewelry anymore because my son pulls at them. But a fun scarf or an all-purpose bag that I love can really help dress up an outfit."

- A great hat: "This is essential to my wardrobe— whether I'm having a bad day or just haven't had the chance to take a shower, a hat can save the day."

Meg's son, Finn, is a constant source of inspiration to her. Below are a few of Meg's favorite items of clothing, including flat-soled boots, a few items from the thrift store, and her Moop bag.

SIMPLICITY IN STYLE

It's interesting for Meg to think about fashion and style. She recently spent three years living and teaching in rural Mexico, where every day she wore jeans and T-shirts for practicality. "I am very influenced by my time in Mexico. I lived on a street with no name and outdoor latrines. I'm very cognizant of that, and ever since I've returned, I have tried even harder to minimize my carbon foot print." It is important to Meg to live comfortably within her means, and to dedicate time to her family. The simple life she aims for is conflicting, however. "I'll get catalogs from beautiful stores like Anthropologie, and I'll want everything in the store," she says.

At home, Meg's style is defined by utilitarianism. "I'm still a nursing mom," says Meg, "so I can't wear cute little belts or certain dresses, although that would be fun." Even though she looks for function in her wardrobe, Meg artistically blends comfort into her style. She loves thrift stores for clothing items, as well as the Gap and Land's End's younger line, Canvas. She also loves to make her own clothes. "My mom was a seamstress, and she taught me how to sew," says Meg. "I've always liked clothes, and I loved that once I knew how to sew I was able to see something I liked and actually go home and re-create it myself. Plus, then I could tweak it to my exact preference."

Meg grew up in Nevada City, California, near the Yuba River. She credits much of her style to that community where people are very artistic and spend much of their time outdoors. She wore a lot more color back then, but she can still see the connection between the place she grew up in and her style today.

1 Meg and her husband both play the guitar, and one of their favorite activities is to make music—while Finn dances and sings along with them. **2** Meg's Montessori background has influenced the type of toys that Finn plays with—she prefers natural materials, like this mini kitchen made from wood. **3** Meg's favorite colors are those found in nature—whether it's sky blue, sunset reds, or pretty greens and browns.

MEG'S PRIZED WEARABLES

- Little brown hat: a sure way to receive a compliment
- Purple and cream scarf that her dearest friend gave her as a birthday present
- Birkenstocks: "I love the Sparta style, and have them in steel blue."
- Black camper boots: "I've had these for years, and they're still going strong."
- The Sunday Picnic Blouse is one of Meg's new patterns, and she has several of them. "I can feel dressed up because it's a wrap dress or shirt, but it still allows me to be a nursing mom."
- Rusty-orange Moop bag
- The Schoolhouse Tunic: "This was part of my first design collection, and I love how it fits."
- Her Emmeline Apron was also part of Meg's first collection, and it's a staple around her house.

SURROUNDED BY INSPIRATION

When Meg experiences a creative block, she knows it's just not her time to be producing. "I can't squeeze creativity out of myself," she says, "so I'll just put that project on the back burner until I get that spark back." For inspiration, she often looks on Flickr or flips through magazines. Her son is also a huge inspiration to her work. "I can't find store-bought pants that will fit a cloth diaper baby," Meg says. "I'm constantly designing clothes for him—anything to help his growth and independence."

Once she is inspired, Meg immediately transfers her ideas to paper. "Whether it's notations or sketches, they go straight to paper," she says. "I have whole design scrapbooks just to keep my notes organized." The actual construction of a garment, or accessory, or home décor item is next, and much of this step is trial and error.

Meg has also created a home environment for harboring inspiration, both for her and her young son. "It's very important to create a living space where adults and children can co-exist, where we

can both move well and with confidence," says Meg. She has little cabinets set aside in each room of her house specifically for Finn and his toys. Many of the walls in Meg's house are a neutral color, and the bright pops of color she has added to each room are similar to the bright colors she adds to the neutral foundation of her wardrobe. "My time in Mexico influenced my already present love of color." Meg's love of nature-inspired color, a simple lifestyle, and her family all contribute to the person she is, and the mark she's already leaving on the world.

MEG CAN'T LIVE WITHOUT

- Her husband: "I couldn't do anything I do without his support."
- Good food and the time to spend making it: "The time to sit down and have meals together really centers our family. That luxury would be a difficult one to live without."
- Access to nature

One of Meg's favorite pieces in her home is the pillow with the modern tree appliqué, which was originally created for her first book. Meg loves that it's eye-catching but not too loud.

PERFECT BABY SHORTS

As a **new mom** of a baby boy, Meg loves having **plenty** of these shorts ready to pull onto her little guy. Not only are they **comfortable** and **durable**, they are stylish.

WHAT YOU'LL NEED

Template (page 140)

Dark solid cotton fabric: ½ yard (45.7 cm)

Thread in coordinating color

½-inch-wide (1.3 cm) elastic—for waist
- 15 inches (40.6 cm) for 12 month, 14½ inches (36.8 cm) for 6 month, 13 inches (33 cm) for 3 month

¼-inch-wide (.6 cm) elastic—two indentical lengths for leg openings
- 8 inches (20.3 cm) for 12 month, 7½ inches (19 cm) for 6 month, 7 inches (17.8 cm) for 3 month

1 Cut the Fabric

With the template on page 140, cut two pieces from a dark solid cotton fabric and use a ¼-inch (.6 cm) seam allowance on all the stitching.

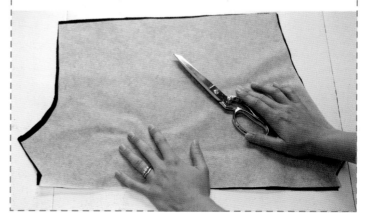

30

2 Stitch the Long Curves

With right sides together, stitch along the long curves.

3 Stitch the Short Curves

Open up seam allowances and stitch along the short curves.

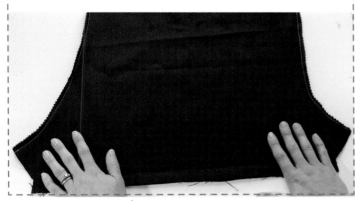

4 Snip Snip

Cut little snips along the stitched short curves.

5 Fold & Stitch Hems & Waist

On both leg hems and at the waist, fold ¼ inch (.6 cm) and then fold ½ inch (1.3 cm) and sew, leaving about a 2-inch (5 cm) opening. Pull through a length of elastic on each of the openings for the legs and a length of elastic through the opening for the waist.

6 Zigzag Stitch the Elastic

When the elastic is pulled all the way through, overlap and secure it with a zigzag stitch. Whipstitch the openings closed. Turn right side out.

ELSIE FLANNIGAN

www.redvelvetart.com
www.abeautifulmess.typepad.com

As a designer, painter, and creator of various handmade items, **Elsie Flannigan** is living out her dreams in Missouri, where she runs her online and local boutique, Red Velvet Art. Bright colors, quirky characters, and all things vintage permeate her store, home, and artwork—and, of course, her personal style.

AN INSTINCTIVE LOVE FOR THRIFTING

Elsie feels she was attracted to similar things as a child as she is now. "I think you are born instinctually to recognize what you love," says Elsie. "For me, I have loved dresses, hats, and gloves for as long as I can remember." Growing up, she went to a small school where she had to wear skirts that went below her knee every day. "That's why I bought thrift-store dresses," she says. "Everyone else had denim, but thrift-store dresses were an early love for me."

Even as a child, there were easy ways for Elsie to be trendy. Her parents were happy with her spending habits, since she bought most everything at thrift stores. Elsie and her sister started thrifting three to four times a week once she had her driver's license. "My parents were open to letting us explore our styles," she says. "My mom even told me to never change my style, even when I grew up."

INSPIRATION FROM FAMILY & FILMS

For Elsie, style is about putting things together—a dress you love, funky handmade accessories, and colorful nail polish. "Fashion is more definable, and easier to label," she says, "whereas style is a mixture of all the things you love." One way Elsie suggests creating your own style is to choose a favorite decade or style, and build off of that. "The details you add to that base can come from anywhere, and can combine in so many different ways."

33

(1) Elsie recently adopted this little pug named Suki, who is now a permanent feature in her studio. **(2)** Elsie loves green apples—she often eats them with cinnamon. **(3)** For those cold and snowy winter days, there's nothing better for Elsie than a cute handmade owl hat. **(4)** Two of her favorite things are foxes and making pillows—so this cute fox family of pillows seems fitting for her home. **(5)** Mini embroidered pieces make perfect small decorations—she often leaves them in the hoop to hang on her wall, and then switches them out whenever she likes.

ELSIE CAN'T LIVE WITHOUT

- Her puppy Suki
- A date with her boyfriend: "We have a lunch and coffee date every day. It's non-negotiable."
- Colored nail polish, which always puts her in a good mood
- Movie theater popcorn
- Fake glasses

ELSIE'S PRIZED WEARABLES

- Silver sparkle cat-eye glasses, given to Elsie by her grandmother, who wore them in high school
- Striped one-piece swimsuit, also given to Elsie by her grandmother
- Catholic memorabilia, including Rosary necklaces, from her grandmother
- Light pink '50s wedding dress
- Dress collection: "I've been growing this collection since high school. And as long as I can stay a size 4, I'll always be able to wear them."

Elsie's boyfriend, whom she affectionately calls "Mr. Larson" on her blog, plays a big part in her life and has inspired several paintings, one of which she used on this pillow.

Elsie's favorite decade is the '60s. "I really like the way the clothes fit," she says, "especially the dresses. I buy a lot of dresses from that era." She also likes accessories and dresses from the '70s. Some of Elsie's favorite places to find clothing from those decades are located right in her city. "There is an amazing vintage store right on my street, and several other trendy shops and flea markets. I also shop online—on Etsy or eBay—as well as at the vintage stores of several of my friends."

Elsie's grandmother is a great inspiration. "She has great style, including a pair of fabulous sparkly glasses." Elsie has loved to see some of the pieces her grandmother has worn over the years. "She keeps everything, and has just boxes of clothes. She gave me some of her clothes from the '60s, including a swimsuit from her honeymoon." The pieces her grandmother gave her are among Elsie's most special vintage belongings.

Elsie's style is also inspired by Betsey Johnson, as well as Mary Blair, who designed for the Walt Disney Company. "She produced concept art for the '60s versions of *Peter Pan* and *Alice in Wonderland*, and she was amazing. She's my number one inspiration."

YEARS OF PLANNING & HARD WORK

Elsie began her blog in 2005, just for fun. "People were starting blogs, and I wanted to do it for a hobby," she says. "Now I've worked on it for so many years that it's become a very big part of my life." Elsie has been working independently since her early twenties. "Every venture takes a lot of time, years of it," she explains. When asked about the key to running a successful business, Elsie points out that it can't happen overnight—there's no automatic solution; it takes constant planning and re-evaluation. "Only then will you have a successful business."

Inspiration plays a large part in both Elsie's blog and business. She is inspired by music, movies, and other artists, particularly painters. "I like to translate what I hear or see into a medium that I'm comfortable working with." Her favorite band is the Flaming Lips, but right now she is also really into Margot & the Nuclear So and So's and Daniel Johnston. "Overall, I like pretty music with pretty words," she says. Movies from Charlie Kaufman, Wes Anderson, and Pixar inspire Elsie as well. "*Up* was really great."

When Elsie is stumped for inspiration, she usually takes a break to go shopping or to a bookstore where she finds different elements that refresh her. "I don't push through it," says Elsie. "I don't think that works. Instead, I get out and find something exciting, then work on translating that into my projects."

It's often a color or a feel that inspires her in these stores. "Pretty stores just make me want to make my store more beautiful," she says. And with a store as beautiful as her style, she's content exactly where she is. "As a kid, I kind of imagined the adult that I wanted to be. One of my happiest thoughts is that who I am today reflects that same person."

ESSENCE OF ELSIE'S STYLE

- Dresses: "Dresses seem easier to use to pull together a look than jeans and a shirt. A dress with a cute pair of tights and shoes, and it's done."

- Big hair: "I love a '60s bump, and definitely consider that part of my style. It's an easy style, which only requires a lot of teasing and hair spray."

- Faux lashes: "It's a seemingly small item, but it can add a lot to your look."

- Colorful painted fingernails

- Handmade clothing items: "Whether it's a small accessory or a whole dress, handmade is so important to me that I seem to always be wearing something that either I've made or one of my friends has made."

- Thrift store pieces

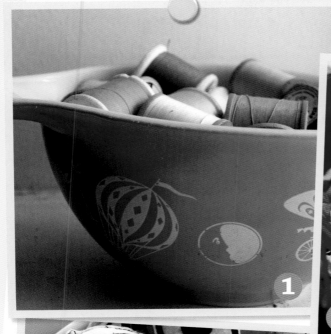

1 Elsie loves vintage Pyrex, and often searches for new pieces on her thrift store runs. 2 Owls are another one of Elsie's favorite animals, and are often used in her artwork. 3 Elsie's stash of vintage buttons helps her add personality to many of her clothing and home décor projects. 4 Elsie's always on the lookout for vintage craft supplies, and fell in love with these pretty red ribbons at first sight.

CHUNKY & LEAFY FELT HEADBAND

Elsie Flannigan is passionate about bamboo and wool felts. She believes such quality materials transform an **ordinary** felt project into an **extraordinary** one.

WHAT YOU'LL NEED

Template (page 141)

Bamboo or wool felt in two colors: 1/8 yard (11.4 cm)

Embroidery floss

Hand needle

Elasticized ribbon: 14 inches (35.6 cm)

1 Cut Leaves & Start Stitching

With the template on page 141, and two contrasting shades of bamboo felt, cut out four leaf shapes. Use a needle with embroidery floss in a contrasting color to start adding large chunky straight stitches at one end of one of the leaves.

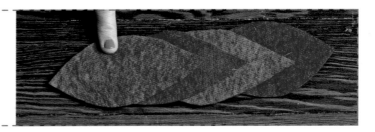

2 ## Add the Second Leaf

After about an inch (2.5 cm) of stitching, layer a second leaf beneath the first leaf and continue stitching together.

4 ## Add the Final Leaf

Add a fourth and final leaf. Of course if you would like your headband to have more than four leaves, you can easily add more. You can also modify the spacing to make the leaves either closer together or farther apart.

3 ## Add the Third Leaf

After about two total inches (5.1 cm) have been stitched, add a third leaf and continue stitching.

5 ## Attach Decorative Elasticized Ribbon

Determine the length needed for your head and use a needle and embroidery floss to attach a length of decorative elasticized ribbon to both ends of the stitched leaves.

RASHIDA COLEMAN-HALE

Rashida Coleman-Hale is the creative genius and sewing artist behind the blog I Heart Linen. With an eye for color that translates so well into countless fabric projects, Rashida is also the author of *I Love Patchwork: 21 Irresistible Zakka Projects to Sew*. Rashida's love of color and quality fabrics extends to her personal style as well, as shown in her wardrobe and in the home she shares with her husband and children.

AN EYE FOR STYLE & COMFORT

For Rashida, style is the ability to combine various items to create a standout look. "It's a skill to not only be able to pick out the right things that look good on you and fit your personality, but to also combine them in a way that works for you," she says. "You really have to have an eye for what will actually complement you, regardless of what may be in fashion."

Rashida doesn't think she had style when she was younger: "As a kid, as with many kids, I just wore what my mom and dad told me to wear." When she reached her adolescent years, she wore what most typical teenagers in the '90s wore—the "grunge" look, and of course the Doc Martens. "It's like I was trying to not fit in, but in doing so I fit in just because that's what everyone else wore, too," she remembers. "By the time I got to college, I was like, 'Wait a minute. This isn't me.'" It was then that she realized she had been trying to fit in all along, and it was also the time that she really started experimenting with different looks. Studying fashion design at the Fashion Institute of Technology influenced her. "I think that played a huge part in discovering who I am and what I like to wear," Rashida says.

Ever since then, she's gone through various phases. "About five years ago, I had a pink phase," she says. "It felt like everything I owned had some type of pink in it, like Pink Panther threw up in my closet. I met my husband during that phase. Let's just say I'm glad I've moved past that." Now, her wardrobe is largely about comfort—with cute mixed in as well. "Now that I have three kids, I want to be stylish, but I also have to be able to run around," says Rashida. "I don't like to wear my best clothes, because there's a good chance they'll get spit up on or spilled on." Rashida looks for clothes that are unique, yet easy to throw on and easy to wash.

41

SURROUNDED BY COLORFUL INSPIRATION

Many things inspire Rashida. "In this day and age there are so many avenues for inspiration," she says. "I get a lot of inspiration from other artists, whether it's on their Flickr streams or blogs." Rashida is also inspired out of pure necessity—for example, she needed a new pillow on her couch, so she immediately made one. That spark can come from a color palette she likes, a magazine she reads, or a button she finds. When she does experience a lack of inspiration, Rashida has a file in her computer of photos she's taken or found. "I just flip through them, look at the colors, and usually it doesn't take long to be inspired again," she says.

Two of Rashida's favorite colors are aqua and yellow. "The combination of the two just makes me melt," she says. "I love the ocean and the beach, and these two colors remind me of that." If she could be anywhere in the world, it would be on the beach, or in the Caribbean—she loves anything that reminds her of those places. "I also love how these two colors go with so many other colors," says Rashida. "Aqua and yellow together go with everything."

WORKING WHILE THEY NAP

Rashida is a stay-at-home mom to three young children, so her routine often consists of cooking, cleaning, story time, trips to the playground, and naptime. Luckily, she manages to have all three of her kids take a nap at the same time, an unusual occurrence for many moms. "Naptime is when I have my 'me' time," says Rashida. "When they're napping, I'll check e-mail, or do a bit of business." Her sewing often doesn't happen until late at night.

When the house is quiet, Rashida will pull out an old movie she hasn't seen before. "I love having old movies on in the background when I'm sewing," she says. When she needs a break from sewing, she loves to paint, particularly with watercolors. She also plays the violin, and loves classical music, which is often playing in the house. And when she needs a break from creating? "I love to goof around with my husband," says Rashida. "I'm a chill person, and I love to just laugh with him."

Rashida keeps a variety of colorful fabrics on hand—when inspiration strikes she is ready. Sometimes, all a bed needs is a personalized linen pillow with fabric embellishments, as seen below.

① The little things speak volumes in Rashida's home, like the quirky Japanese objects and glass containers that hold her supplies. **②** These patchwork mini-quilts contain aqua and yellow—Rashida's favorite color palette—as well as linen, of course. **③** Rashida loves that her house features a mix of items—everything from wood furniture to vintage items to cutesy accents. **④** When getting dressed, Rashida looks to her collection of shoes in assorted hues to help complete her signature look.

THE ESSENCE OF RASHIDA'S STYLE

- Comfort: "I'm all about comfort, especially now that I'm busy with my kids all the time."

- Casual chic: "I love that look."

- Dresses: "Dresses are so easy to wear, plus they can be dressed up or dressed down easily."

- Flat shoes

A particularly busy time in Rashida's life came when she was writing her book, *I Love Patchwork: 21 Irresistible Zakka Projects to Sew*. "I had two kids at the time," says Rashida, "and we were moving from Manhattan to the suburbs in New Jersey right when my manuscript was due." Rashida didn't get much sleep then because there was always so much to do and write. "But you just make it work when you're that busy," she says, "because you have to make it happen somehow."

With determination and a passion for her craft, Rashida has definitely left her stitch on the world.

This Pretty Patchwork Tote incorporates square patches in her **favorite colors** and plenty of her favorite fabric: **linen.**

PRETTY PATCHWORK TOTE

WHAT YOU'LL NEED

Templates (page 143)

Stash fabric (coordinating patterned cotton in yellows and blues)

Batting: ½ yard (45.7 cm)

Interfacing

Linen: ½ yard (45.7 cm)

Lining fabric (light colored cotton): ½ yard (45.7 cm)

Thread in coordinating color

Rotary cutter & cutting mat

Quilter's ruler

Seam Allowance:
¼-inch (.6 cm) for piecing small squares;
½-inch (1.3 cm) all else

1 Piece Together Squares

With coordinating fabrics, cut 54 fabric squares that measure 2½ x 2½ inches (6.4 x 6.4 cm). Piece together two panels, with three rows of nine squares. Once pieced, layer the segments with batting. Cut additional squares to create straps by piecing squares in like fashion, then adding interfacing, and stitching together with strips of linen.

2 Cut Linen for the Bag's Bottom

With the lower half template on page 143, cut two pieces of linen for the lower body of the bag. (Be sure to mark all notches.) Use the same template to cut two pieces of batting. Place each linen piece on top of each batting piece.

3 Tuck & Sew

Use the two notch marks on the left side as guides to tuck fabric at each notch mark toward the left by ¼ inch (.6 cm) and pin. Use the two notch marks on the right side as guides to tuck fabric at each notch mark toward the right by ¼ inch (.6 cm) and pin. Back tack at these tucks, using a ¼-inch (.6 cm) seam allowance.

4 Sew Top & Bottom Together

Stitch both the top and bottom pieces for both sides of the bag. Then with right sides together, pin the two sides of the bag together, and sew along the side edges, leaving the bottom open.

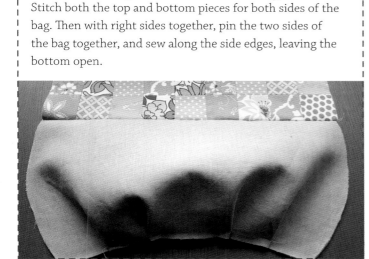

5 Prepare the Bottom

Use the bottom template on page 143 to cut one piece for the bag's bottom with linen. Cut a piece of batting the same size and stitch together along the edges.

6 Stitch the Bottom to the Bag

With right sides together, pin the bag's bottom to the body of the bag and sew. Cut small snips along the sewn bottom to allow the bottom to open up when turned right side out.

7 Sew the Lining

Pin the handles to the bag with right sides together. With the lining template, and using lining fabric of your choice, cut two pieces and also a bottom piece with the bottom template. Sew a lining bag in like fashion as the main bag.

8 Sew the Lining to the Bag

Encase the bag with the lining with right sides together. Pin and sew along the top edge, leaving a small section open. Turn the bag right side out and whipstitch the opening closed.

KATHY CANO-MURILLO

www.craftychica.com
www.thecraftychica.blogspot.com

Kathy Cano-Murillo is a writer, artist, and craft product designer. She has sold her Chicano Pop Art crafts and products to hundreds of retailers, including Bloomingdales, Target, and Michaels. She has authored several books, including *Crafty Chica's Guide to Artful Sewing*, *Waking Up in the Land of Glitter*, and *Miss Scarlet's School of Patternless Sewing*. Kathy has also appeared in several newspapers and on several websites across the country—all while maintaining her style that exudes craft, drama, and glitter.

ARTFUL & EMOTIONAL STYLE

Kathy remembers being in grade school and living at home in a conservative, Mexican-American household. Her next-door neighbor was the daughter of the famous artist Ted DeGrazia. "She was a mom with kids, but she was always dripping in noisy costume jewelry," says Kathy. "She wore bright muumuus and always dressed like she was going to a cocktail party on a cruise ship. I was so intrigued." Kathy often asked to go shopping with her neighbor, and because her neighbor's own daughters didn't like her style, she adopted Kathy as her style buddy. "She'd buy me charm bracelets and crazy necklaces," Kathy says. "I knew then that I loved heavy, loud pieces of jewelry—and that I wanted to wear them all at the same time."

Ever since then, Kathy has been into finding one-of-a-kind pieces to wear as the focal point of her outfits, and then accessorizing around those pieces. Kathy always has on at least one item that makes her feel artful and sexy. "I'm plus-size but refuse to fall into the baggy clothing trap," she says. "I refuse to be frumpy." Kathy is not a less-is-more kind of person. Instead, she feels that it's important that everything she wears and creates has a story to tell. "We live our lives with lots of emotion, and what we make and wear should be a reflection of that."

LIVING & BREATHING INSPIRATION

Just being alive inspires Kathy. "I make the most of breathing, seeing, tasting, hearing, touching," she says. "Art is a way to document all of that." Kathy tries to make every single day an eventful, romantic, and memorable one. The cultures of Jamaica and the Caribbean also inspire Kathy, as well as reggae music. Her favorite three-color combination is red, yellow, and green. "In Jamaica, they see these colors as red representing the blood of life, yellow representing the sun, and green representing the land," says Kathy. "These colors make me happy."

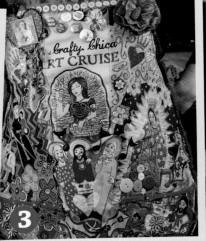

① Kathy begins each morning with a kiss and an "I love you" to her husband, some computer time, and an iced coffee. ② Kathy loves accessories, like these colorful hoop earrings. ③ Kathy tends to have a lot of busy layers in her work, because there are a lot of busy layers in her life.

THE ESSENCE OF KATHY'S STYLE

- Solid foundations
- Dark slacks and expressive tops
- Bright colors
- Balanced look
- Accessories: "I think accessories are the glitter of an outfit."
- Handmade items: "I always wear something handmade, hopefully to spark conversation because I love talking about crafts."

Back in the day, Kathy worked in the music industry, booking bands into nightclubs. She felt empowered to have that kind of job. "It was mostly Caribbean and Jamaican bands, but being a Chicana, I found ways to recruit bands with a sexy, worldbeat vibe for the nightclubs," says Kathy. "I loved the feeling of walking into a room knowing people were watching me." In dressing up for the events, she often felt like she was a walking canvas. Those experiences and cultures still inspire her today. "These days, I take those memories and channel them into the characters I create for my novels," she says.

Movies also inspire Kathy. "I love movies. I have a whole collection that I call 'Crafty Cinema.'" Kathy watches this collection while she works in her studio. Even though she's seen them many times, just hearing the voices inspires her. *White Oleander*, *How to Make an American Quilt*, and *Real Women Have Curves* are all part of this collection. Kathy's also big on inspiration walls. Though many people only have one inspiration board, Kathy has one in every room. "It wasn't planned that way," she says. "That's just the kind of person I am. I'm inspired by so many things, so I make sure to surround myself with them."

Kathy loves to write, whether it's in preparation for an upcoming novel, a blog post, or for her own personal enjoyment.

CRAZY TIMES OF LIFE

One of Kathy's favorite things to do is write about certain crazy scenarios that take place during the day, as if they were part of a sitcom. "I blog about these so that years down the road I'll read them and laugh." She's been blogging since 2003; her kids were little then, and she loves to go back and read those posts about silly tantrums they threw and how she dealt with it. "I won't spend hours creating a beautiful scrapbook page," she says, "but I will sit down and spend an hour writing the play-by-play of the day."

Kathy also loves to doodle. Her doodling is a good example of her constant multi-tasking. Her life has always been busy, so she's figured out how to quickly move back and forth between commitments. When she worked as an entertainment reporter, her movie star phone interviews came at all hours of the day and night. "One time I had to teach at a high-profile workshop and Kurt Russell called right in the middle of it. How do you say no to Kurt Russell?" says Kathy. So she put the phone on speaker and conducted the interview while her class listened and worked on their projects.

Another crazy time of her life came when she had four months to write a novel during the busy art season. "It was very stressful, but I just kept telling myself that I had to do my best and finish in a fabulous way. I knew I would get through it, like I always did, so I stayed focused and concentrated on the finish line. I took it day by day. No, actually, hour by hour."

Kathy often thinks about why she works so hard. "I pinpointed that I started doing it all to impress my parents, to earn their respect. I always felt like the goofy middle child, always average, nothing special." Kathy had visions of winning huge, fancy awards and having her parents jump up and down and hug her because they were so proud and amazed. "But as I grew older," she says, "I realized that awards, headlines, and fame don't impress the way daily doses of love and affection do. That is where true respect comes from." These days, Kathy creates to celebrate life, to show gratitude, and to inspire others to do the same.

THE CRAFTY CHICA'S JUMBO TOTE

This bag was inspired by two **scarves** that Kathy bought at the **dollar store**. At first, Kathy thought of simply stitching them together, but then decided to go all the way and make a jumbo tote for her **crafty adventures**.

WHAT YOU'LL NEED

Scarves (2): 22-inch square (55.9 cm)

Fabric for lining & side and bottom panels: 1¼ yards (114.3 cm)

Thread in coordinating color

Purchased or recycled straps (2): 1¼ x 30-inch (3.2 x 76.2 cm)

Grosgrain ribbon, 5/8 inches (1.6 cm) wide: 60 inches (152.4 cm)

Seam Allowance: ¼-inch (.6 cm)

1 Cut & Sew Side & Bottom Strips

Select two colorful square scarves with a nice focal image. Select a coordinating fabric and cut two squares exactly the same size as the scarves. Cut six additional strips from the coordinating fabric: the strips should each measure your desired width and should be the same length as one side of your square scarf. With right sides together, sew the side strip to the bottom strip and to the other side strip. Repeat this process for the lining strips.

2 Sew the Strips

With right sides together, sew the stitched lining strip segments along the side, bottom, and other side of one of the square scarves. Stitch the second scarf in like fashion to this. At this point, you have created the exterior of the bag. Repeat this entire process to create the lining for the bag with the previously cut fabric.

3 Position the Handles

With either purchased or handmade straps, pin the ends of the handles to the top edge of the bag's exterior.

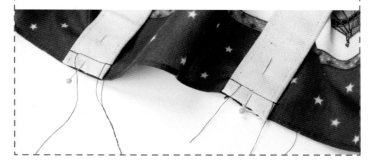

4 Sew the Lining to the Bag

Drop the lining into the exterior bag with right sides facing. Pin and sew (with a back tack at the beginning and end) along the top edge of the bag. Be sure to leave a 4-inch (10.2 cm) hole to use to turn the bag right side out.

5 Topstitch the Handles

Once the bag is turned right side out, add topstitching to reinforce the handles.

6 Add the Ribbon

Zigzag stitch a length of grosgrain ribbon on the interior top edge of the bag for added reinforcement.

7 Add Topstitching

Add topstitching along the seam lines of the entire bag for added reinforcement.

51

BETZ WHITE

www.betzwhite.com
blog.betzwhite.com

Betz White has built a career on thoughtful design and skilled craftsmanship with a focus on materials that are kind to people and planet alike. She is an author, designer, and crafter who often uses secondhand materials as the basis for her projects. Her creations have a bright and whimsical style that can be seen in her home, her wardrobe, and her designs.

EARLY CREATIVITY IN STYLE

Betz grew up in a family of creative souls. "They always encouraged me to be artistic and explore my creativity." One of Betz's earliest memories includes coloring the toes of her saddle shoes; she didn't want just black-and-white shoes, so she colored the white parts red. She also dressed up often as a child, and role-playing was one of her favorite activities. "I would wear shoes and glasses that belonged to my mom," she says, "and I would instantly become Mrs. McGillicuddy." Amusingly enough, "Mrs. McGillicuddy" was a name Betz wanted to use for a children's wear line.

Betz's grandma would always comment on the crazy things Betz wore growing up. "She actually told me at a young age that I should go to fashion-design schoool, but I didn't listen then." Eventually, Betz ended up right where her grandmother said she would. "She had a vision for me even before I realized it." Her grandma influenced her in more ways than one; she taught Betz to "waste not, want not." Her grandma was a great example of buying quality items. "She always told me that if I was going to spend money on clothes, then I should just buy a few really nice things."

53

Boots make a frequent appearance in Betz's wardrobe. Whether they're her comfortable Frye boots or her red rain boots, they're all about function and style.

A WARDROBE ALL HER OWN

Betz's style evolved over the years, from preppy in high school to new wave punk, to the days when her dad would just shake his head when she walked downstairs in the morning. "But my parents never discouraged me from experimenting," she says.

Now, her style has been changed by practicality. "I'm older, with kids," she says, "and my style has had to shift and adjust to that." Another factor that affects her dress is working from home. "If I worked in a corporate world and didn't have kids, my wardrobe would be different," she says. But the way her schedule is structured, she frequently works for an entire day without seeing a single person.

Though the practical side often wins out, Betz admires the styles of people she comes in contact with. "I think building my own style has had a lot to do with what I've seen on other people. It's choosing pieces of someone else's style that speak to you, and making them your own."

1 One of Betz's favorite ways to relax is to knit, which allows her to be creative in a completely different way from her everyday work. **2** Bright colors permeate both Betz's pattern lines and personal style, as shown here with one of her favorite pairs of shoes.

THE ESSENCE OF BETZ'S STYLE

- Function more than purely looks
- Fun with colors or mixing patterns
- A touch of fun, even on a small scale: "Even when I'm wearing something simple, I love to add a big turquoise ring or other unique accessory to make it fun."

FLUID WORKDAY & HOME LIFE

With a family and a growing business, Betz's days are busy. "Though I don't know how exciting they are," she says. Betz is always up before her two kids, ideally with enough time to write a few e-mails—though getting up that early is challenging, especially with two boys who are often awake really early. "Our schedules vary depending on whether or not the boys are in school. Summers are a different story around here, as I spend more time with the kids then." Normally, her days consist of getting the boys off to school, after which she has the whole day to work. "Once they're home from school, I go into Mom mode again, with dinner, homework, and putting the boys to bed." Once the boys are in bed, Betz works again for a while, then ends the day by spending time with her husband. "At the end of every day I also make a to-do list for the next day," she says. "If I don't do this, I'm lost the next day."

WORLD OF MISSONI

1 Betz loves to use up every scrap in her work, so she often makes flowers with the smallest pieces of felt. **2** Items that were handed down to Betz from her family, along with found objects, contribute to her eclectic style. **3** Betz keeps both old sweaters and fabric on hand to use in her work. **4** Betz's inspiration board is filled with cards and swatches in her favorite colors.

BETZ'S PRIZED WEARABLES

- Favorite jeans: "Which totally depends on the minute."
- Frye harness boots: "I wear these whenever I can. They are stylish, and comfortable, and just cool."
- Orla Kiely sweater with orange polka dots
- Hand-knit hats and scarves
- Charm bracelet that contains charms her grandma collected throughout her life
- Necklace that her husband made out of a vacuum tube and found objects

Betz has a fluid workday, moving between writing for magazines, working on long-term assignments, like designing new fabric lines, and sewing. She likes to work on assignments with hard deadlines in the morning when she's most focused.

When Betz has some time to spend on activities she enjoys, she loves to knit. "It uses a different part of the brain than I'm used to relying on all day," she says. "Knitting is soothing and repetitive for me, especially when I'm sitting by the lake on vacation." Betz also really loves to make things with her family, whether they're at a local pottery class or right at home in her studio. She also volunteers in her kids' art classes, which helps break up her workday and gives her the chance to see how her kids are doing in school.

Whether it's spending time with her family, sewing, or exploring her creativity, Betz's style is uniquely bright, functional, and fun—traits she carries throughout her entire body of work.

BETZ CAN'T LIVE WITHOUT

- Family and nature
- Fresh air and natural light
- Coffee and chocolate
- Mascara and lip balm

Betz creates small animals out of felt scraps, some of which end up as toys for her two young sons. Here she wears one of her favorite sweaters—simple, but with color and personality, just the way Betz likes it.

57

LETTUCE-EDGE CASHMERE SHRUG

This project requires one cashmere sweater, either a cardigan or pullover that generally fits you—**not too loose** but not too tight. (The following steps are written for a **pullover** but it's easy enough to adapt for a **cardigan.)**

WHAT YOU'LL NEED

Cashmere sweater

Ruler

Hand needle

Thread in coordinating color

1 Measure & Cut

Try on the sweater and decide where you would like the bottom edge of the shrug to hit, probably somewhere close to your natural waistline. Mark the length with a pin. Take off the sweater and mark this measurement with pins across the width. Cut across the width of the sweater through both layers. Set aside the long piece to be used later for the tie.

2 Cut the Center

Cut the center front from the bottom edge to the neckline, cutting through the front layer of the sweater only.

3 Remove the Collar & Create the Neckline

If the sweater has a collar, cut it off at the neckline. Lay a ruler, from the bottom edge to the side of the neckline, and mark the angle with pins. Cut along the pin line to open up the neckline like a V. To copy the angle on the other side of the neckline, lay the piece that was cut away on top of the other side and cut following the edge.

4 Create the Tie

Use the length of scrap removed in step 1, and cut off ⅓ of the length to use as the short tie. The other ⅔ will be used as the long tie. The width of the tie should be no wider than 4 inches (10.2 cm). Open up the front of the shrug and pin the short tie to the wearer's right; pin the long tie to the wearer's left, right sides together. Sew ties to the front, removing the pins. Trim the unsewn ends of the tie by cutting at a 45° angle. Make a small slit in the side seam at the wearer's left for the tie to pass through, about one inch (2.5 cm) up from the edge.

5 Cut the Sleeves

Try on the shrug and tie, pulling the short tie through the slit and wrapping the long tie to the right and around the back to the other side. Mark the desired sleeve length with a pin. Take the shrug off and cut off excess sleeve length. Copy the length on the other side and cut. Create a lettuce edge by sewing a zigzag stitch around the cut edge of each sleeve while gently stretching the fabric.

6 Make the Rosette

Cut a 1½-inch-wide (3.8 cm) strip about 6–8 inches (15.2–20.3 cm) long from the leftover sleeve scraps. Lettuce edge one side by using a zigzag stitch and gently stretching the fabric at the same time. With a needle and thread, run a basting stitch along the other edge of the strip. Pull threads to gather. Roll the strip, then stitch the gathered edges together to keep the rosette securely rolled. Cut two leaves if desired, and "lettuce" the edges as you did on the sleeves. Hand sew the rosette and leaves to the front of the shrug where the long tie is attached.

MEG ALLAN COLE

Meg Allan Cole is a hard-working, sustainable-design maven who creates innovative content for Etsy, Craft:zine, and her blog, Nest. Meg is also founder of Enderby—her unique line of handmade clothing. You can also view Meg's videos and blog posts on Threadbanger's Décor It Yourself pages. With her family and dogs by her side, Meg confidently shows off her style in all facets of her life.

A BALANCING ACT

Meg Allan Cole begins each day drinking organic coffee with her husband and their two rescue mutts. "This is a much-needed quiet and loving start to the busy day," explains Meg. Every day is different, and she is still trying to find the balance for her three-tiered career. She has certain days for different projects. Mondays, Tuesdays, and Wednesday mornings are all Décor It Yourself days, and Wednesday afternoons and Thursdays are for Enderby, Nest, correspondence, and planning quality online content for magazines and resource centers.

"My husband juggles just as much as I do with his job as a web developer, his indie record label and band, and his freelance work, and I think we are a good team," says Meg. "We help each other out on really busy days, and we each know how to get the other to relax and chill." Meg and her husband are strict about making sure they have a couple of nights a week together. They find that downtime as absolutely crucial for their balance. She also balances the business aspect of her life by walking her dogs, going to the gym, listening to records, participating in a weekly bowling league, and training for Bike MS NYC—the large cycling event that raises support to fight multiple sclerosis.

61

1 One of Meg's favorite things to do is explore Brooklyn, especially in the company of her dogs. **2** Much of her collection of brooches comes from her Nana, who loved big baubles with rhinestones. **3** Meg loves white or otherwise neutral backgrounds, so more vibrant hues, and some of her favorite colors, like celadon green and mustard, can stand out.

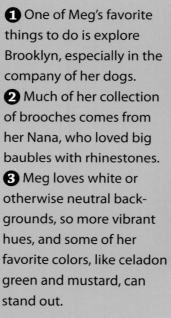

THE ESSENCE OF MEG'S STYLE

- Vintage, vintage, vintage: Many clothing items from the '60s and '70s are pieces Meg would wear today.

- Sentimental pieces of clothing, like those passed down from her grandmothers and mother

- Bright colors

- Funky accessories, whether it's an interesting belt that pulls a vintage dress together or a chunky necklace in a bright color

Meg's style, as evidenced by her clothes seen here, has been influenced by her Oma's collection of vintage dresses, as well as the fantastically retro vibe of stylist Barret Wertz, who also happens to be one of her very best friends.

FINDING INSPIRATION AT HOME

Meg lives in New York City. One of the things she finds so incredible about it is that art is everywhere. She finds inspiration just walking through the streets of her neighborhood. Meg thinks of Williamsburg, Brooklyn, as an outdoor museum and an ever-changing canvas for local artists. If she needs more inspiration beyond her locale, she flips through books on Avedon of the '60s, Frank Lloyd Wright, Cindy Sherman, Amy Sedaris, Andy Warhol, or The Beatles. She also listens to records by David Bowie, Velvet Underground, Pulp, or The Pixies. And if none of those usual avenues for inspiration work? "I take some deep breaths and leave it until I'm ready."

As someone who spends much of the day gathering inspiration and working from home, Meg realizes how a home is a canvas for the art of living. "It's like a time capsule of your life and should be filled with all that is you and all that is your life," says Meg. Some of the relics in her home that she could not live without are her Nana's colored glass collection, her Papa's typewriter, a wooden lamp her dad hand carved in shop class, *The Giving Tree* with an inscription from her mom when Meg was five, the mod-pod ottoman from her Oma, her Mummum's recipe collection, and the collection of vintage purses that goes back generations from the women in her mom's, stepmom's, and mother-in-law's families.

63

Meg's dark blue dress lends itself beautifully to the funky belt and chunky gold jewelry she uses to accessorize. Meg loves her capelet, shown below, which she says is the perfect design to be made out of the yards of vintage fabric that belonged to her Nana.

ROCKING HER PERSONAL STYLE

From perms and scrunchies and Docs and jeans, to vintage mod frocks and funky accessories, Meg's style has continuously evolved. "There are so many hilarious incarnations of what I thought was stylish," she explains. "Some were lovely, some were mostly funny, some were embarrassing...and some are pieces I would still totally rock today."

Since she was a little girl, Meg has always been into fashion, style, and everything aesthetically pleasing. "When you have your own personal style, I think it absolutely reflects in your fashion. Embracing your natural style means not having to try so hard. Just embracing who you are and what you like, and not having to apologize for either." Meg has always known what she loves, and what isn't for her. She credits her mom and Nana for being supportive as she searched for her own style. "Even as a teenager, heading

out to a show with a shirt that had flames going up the sleeves, they got a kick out of my ability to express myself through fashion," says Meg. Their encouragement and freedom helped her hone her emerging style and embrace her individuality.

Meg loves people who can bring their personal touch to every piece they own. "Your style should be all about you," she says. "Knowing who you are, what and who you love, what hits you on a gut level, what culture you connect with—all of these are elements of you, and will reflect in your style," shares Meg. Her example of staying true to her own personal style shows just how great embracing who you are can be.

MEG'S PRIZED WEARABLES

- Her mom's vintage London Fog trench coat, circa mid-'70s

- Her Oma's 1950s blue print summer dress: With the collar popped and a belt to cinch the waist, it's a timeless piece.

- Slouchy, oversized gray T-shirt from Muji: It hangs perfectly and is such a great staple with skinny jeans and anything from white Vans to heels or boots.

- Mustard suede wedge booties from Pink Studio: They made Meg start her blog because they were so perfect. She has literally worn them to death.

- Hammered gold hoop earrings, a birthday gift from her mom who found them when traveling in Zurich, Switzerland

- Black suspenders and vintage gray vest

- Rebecca Turbow's Safe grey gardens top: "Love it, love it, love it."

① Meg loves to draw, sketch, and create with oil paints and charcoal. The prints and décor in her home often serve as her inspiration. **②** Here Meg is sporting her favorite black suspenders, the perfect accessory to bring an entire outfit together. **③** Meg has always loved earrings, so much so that she sometimes adds them to a silver choker for a dressed-up necklace. **④** Meg's favorite colors include aqua, poppy, and bubblegum pink—combining them with a neutral color like white feels clean, crisp, and modern to her.

65

ROCKIN' RETRO CAPELET

Meg created her first cape for Enderby Designs, her eco-minded company, a few years ago. She loves using **vintage fabric** to create a **modern** capelet.

WHAT YOU'LL NEED

Templates (page 142)

Red fabric: 1¼ yards (114.3 cm)

Pinking shears

Thread in coordinating color

Black fabric strips (2): 2½ x 16-inch (6.4 x 40.6 cm)

Seam Allowance: ½-inch (1.3 cm)

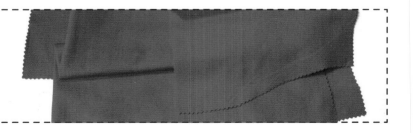

1 Cut the Fabric

Use the template on page 142 and pinking shears to cut one back piece and two front pieces from red fabric. With the hood template on page 142 and using pinking shears, cut two pieces for the hood.

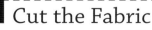

2 Sew the Pieces Together

With right sides together, pin and sew the two front pieces to the back piece. With right sides together, pin and sew the two pieces for the hood.

3 Add Contrasting Topstitching

Use contrasting thread to add topstitching along all sewn lines.

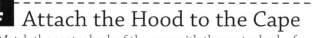

4 Attach the Hood to the Cape

Match the center back of the cape with the center back of the hood. With right sides together, pin and stitch the pieces together.

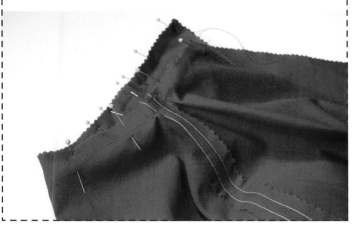

5 Finish the Edges

Fold under all raw edges and finish with topstitching.

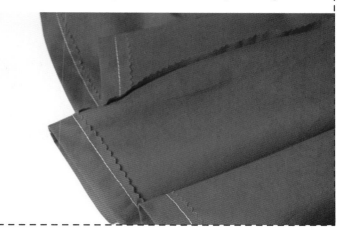

6 Create the Fabric Ties

Cut strips of fabric in a contrasting color according to a width and length that you desire. Fold by a third on one side lengthwise. Fold the other third toward the first fold and stitch down the middle.

7 Sew the Fabric Ties

Sew the fabric ties onto the hood portion to complete.

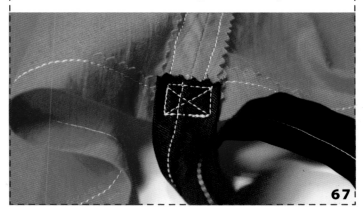

BARI J.
ACKERMAN

As a sewing artist, pattern creator, and fabric designer, **Bari J. Ackerman** knows the importance of great style. She has written a book titled *Inspired to Sew* because she truly is inspired to sew every day of her life. Bari's line of sewing patterns is called *Keeping It Real Sewing Patterns*, and her three fabric lines are called Full Bloom, Art Journal, and Country Lane.

FOR THE LOVE OF HISTORY & DETAILS

During her childhood, Bari was attracted to anything old. "I think I was influenced by my mother. "She and I picked out a chintz printed wallpaper for my room, which I loved and still wish I had." Bari has always felt like she had her own style, even though it may not have been clearly defined in her younger days. "When I was younger, my style was often based on who I wanted people to think I was rather than who I really was," she says. Bari was all about preppy in her early teens, and she loved trendier pieces as she got older. "I was still figuring it out," says Bari. "I don't think I really understood which direction I wanted to go until I was much older."

She was in her late twenties when she really went back to loving historical items. And that's when her clothing style took a more artsy bend. "I think I've really only just grown into my style in the past eight to ten years," says Bari. "And there's something special and almost magical about turning 40. I've only just become who I am." Now, Bari would say that her style is artsy and creative, and embellishments are central to how she dresses. "Ruffles, appliqués, brooches, and interesting details on clothing are what really make me smile." In fact, her love for details led her to make things herself. "I puttered with everything from jewelry made from found objects to collage art and finally to sewing, all in the name of those unbeatable details."

Looking at Bari's style today, it's apparent that her early love for details and embellishments has influenced her lifelong style, which Bari believes is the outward expression of your inner thoughts, feelings, and personality. "I think a person has great style when you can see who they are and what they love just by looking at them," she says.

1 Embellishments are central to the way Bari dresses, including the appliqués she often adds to her clothing. **2** Peonies are one of Bari's favorite flowers—she loves how beautiful they are at every stage of their life. **3** Bari makes and sells these patchwork belts, which combine her love of fabrics and her longstanding love of personalized accessories.

THE ESSENCE OF BARI'S STYLE

- Layering: "I love to put on something lacy underneath shirts, with a little peeking out at the top or the bottom."
- One focal point, so she doesn't overdo it with too many statement pieces
- Vintage items with a modern twist
- Handmade embellishments
- Pops of color, like red shoes with jeans and a plain T-shirt

Bari finds inspiration from items big and small within her surroundings—including her personal china collection, Iris by Nikko, a historical pattern by William Morris.

A SYSTEM OF PRIORITIES

Recently, Bari was finishing her third fabric line, creating a line of patterns, and working on her book all at the same time. "Managing it meant simply writing a list and prioritizing each item by writing an A, B, or C next to it, with the A next to the top priority items," says Bari. "This system doesn't always work, but it keeps me relatively on track." When she's feeling extremely busy, Bari blogs some of her goals, which tends to keep her honest—once she's told everyone she's going to do something, she feels accountable to follow through.

On a daily basis, Bari wakes up early and takes her children to school, followed by a quick workout and a stop for coffee at Peet's Coffee & Tea. Once she's home, she gets to work sewing, designing fabric and patterns, filling orders, doing paperwork, or completing whatever else is on her list of the day. "After I pick the kids up from school there's a lot of running around with them," Bari says, "but after dinner I often pick up right where I left off in the studio."

With Bari working so much of the day, it's imperative for her that she remains inspired and ready to go. Experiences from her childhood, places she loves, things in nature, and color are her major inspirations. "I also tend to daydream about places where I'd like to go, but have never been." If she's at a loss where to start with a fabric design, she just starts doodling. She also tears pictures with inspirational textures, objects, and colors out of magazines.

71

BARI'S PRIZED WEARABLES

- Not Your Daughter's jeans: "They look and feel really great, and I will admit they feel like sweatpants."
- Red patent leather shoes
- Jacket/blazer that is a tone-on-tone damask print in light and dark blue
- Jean skirt
- Brown knee-high riding boots with worn-out leather
- Age-old jeans from J. Jill with embroidery on the bottom of the legs
- Lavender silk dress made from a vintage Vogue pattern by her friend Janis
- A-line lamb shearling jacket with mink collar and three-quarter-length sleeves that was made by her grandfather: "The label inside says 'Furs by Danny' and it belonged to my great-aunt Anne. It is probably my most prized possession."

① Bari's favorite colors are bright pastels, like the green, pink, and yellow shown in this piece. **②** Bari loves her collection of vintage brooches, buttons, and jewelry. **③** Bari often uses vintage brooches to accent her bags, which she sells on her website.

BARI CAN'T LIVE WITHOUT

- Eyeshadow and lipstick
- Aveda Volumizing Tonic
- Hair dryer and round brush
- Good books
- Sewing machine

HAPPY COLORS & NOSTALGIC COLLECTIONS

Bright pastels tend to be Bari's favorite colors. "They're happy colors," she says simply. "I'm one of those people who needs light, with blinds and curtains open and lights on—I think this is why yellow is one of my favorite colors." In fact, one of Bari's favorite pieces in her living room is a chenille-covered settee in butter yellow.

Bari also adores her two slipcovered, lady-like chairs that are in the same room. In her studio, she loves her ever-changing inspiration board, as well as her collections of vintage milk glass, vintage tins, and tons of buttons and brooches. "Something about old items—the nostalgia, the feeling of a simpler time— really speaks to me. It's almost like reaching back and touching the life that our grandparents and great-grandparents lived," says Bari. It's no wonder that pieces from her ancestors' past would speak to her. After all, she thinks that the best way to have great style is to be yourself, and your ancestors are part of who you are. "I know it sounds trite," says Bari, "but it really is true that when you're comfortable with yourself, it doesn't matter how you're dressed—a style shines through."

Bari's inspiration board stays in her studio, but the contents constantly rotate, depending on her projects and ideas. It's decorated with fabrics and objects in her favorite colors and is ever-changing. Here, Bari wears a brightly colored cardigan and makes the outfit her own with one of her signature handmade bags.

73

This **patchwork** zipper pouch was created by Bari to be used as a **makeup bag** as it's the **perfect size** for holding those small essentials.

PERFECTLY PIECED CLUTCH

WHAT YOU'LL NEED

Stash fabric (bright florals & patterns in coordinating colors)

Lining fabric (light colored cotton): ¼ yard (22.9 cm)

Thread in coordinating color

Quilter's ruler

Rotary cutter

Cutting mat

Fusible fleece: ¼ yard (22.9 cm)

Zipper: 12-inch (30.5 cm)

1 Cut & Piece

Gather fabric strips that are 8½ inches (21.6 cm) long and at least 2 inches (5 cm) wide or wider. Use a ¼-inch (.6 cm) seam allowance and then use a quilter's ruler, rotary cutter, and cutting mat to trim piece to measure 12½ x 8½ inches (31.8 x 21.6 cm). Cut a piece of coordinating fabric, two pieces of fusible fleece, and two pieces of lining fabric the same size.

2 Fuse & Fussy Cut

Fuse the fleece to the wrong side of both the patchwork piece and the back panel piece of fabric. Fussy cut a floral motif from fabric, pin it onto the pieced panel, and either appliqué or free motion quilt in place. (NOTE: To fussy cut is to target and cut a specific motif that is printed on the fabric.)

74

3 ## Place the Zipper in Place

With the zipper right side up, place it on top of the right side of the lining pieces, and then place the patchwork panel piece on top with its right side facing the zipper and its wrong side up.

4 ## Sew the Layers Together

With the zipper foot on your machine, sew the three layers together. (Hint: Getting past the zipper pull can sometimes be tricky. Slow down as you approach it and work the zipper behind the foot to continue sewing past it.)

5 ## Repeat Steps 3 & 4

Repeat steps 3 & 4 for the other side of the zipper and the outside back panel and its coordinating lining. Mark a line 1½ inches (3.8 cm) from the tip of the triangle. Sew across the line and then trim the excess fabric triangle off the end.

6 ## Position the Lining

With the zipper unzipped, bring both sides of the lining to one side, right sides together, and both sides of the outer fabric to the other side, right sides together. The zipper teeth should be facing toward the lining side. (Double check that the zipper is open or you won't be able to turn the project once sewn together.)

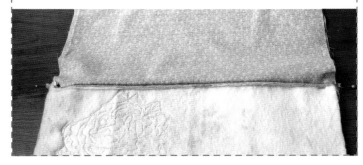

7 ## Sew & Turn

Sew along all sides leaving a 3-inch (7.6 cm) opening in the center of the bottom of the lining to turn. Make sure you sew on the outside of the metal ends of the zipper.

8 ## Create the Flat Bottom

To create a flat bottom, press the seams open, and push one side seam down until it is directly on top of the bottom seam, creating a triangle at the bottom corner of the bag.

9 ## Sew & Trim

Mark a line 1½ inches (3.8 cm) from the tip of the triangle. Sew across the line and then trim the excess fabric triangle off the end.

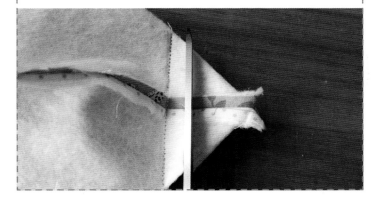

10 ## Repeat Steps 8 & 9

Repeat steps 8 and 9 for the other bottom corner of the bag and both lining bottom corners. Carefully edge stitch the opening in the lining closed, using a ⅛-inch (.3 cm) seam allowance. Tuck the lining into the clutch.

ERIKA & MONIKA SIMMONS
the Double Stitch Twins

The hand-crocheted apparel that has become synonymous with the Double Stitch Twins is a reflection of the twins themselves: fun, flirty, not limited by a certain color palette, and one of a kind. **Erika and Monika Simmons** create out-of-this-world crocheted pieces, and often combine them with fabric for their signature re-mix style—their unmistakable creations can't help but turn heads.

STYLISH SET OF TWINS

Erika and Monika have always felt that they had their own style. Even if their style hasn't always reflected the current fashion, they have always believed that feeling good about their personal look is more important than following trends. "As young children, we would wear two different colors of socks, oversized blazers that we got from thrift stores, as well as fashionable pieces that matched current trends."

Their ease with personal style began in their youth. "We lived in a household with a big sister who had a very defined sense of style, which didn't in any way include the way we dressed. We had to be pretty strong to go up against, 'You can't wear that with that' all the time." Erika and Monika say that if they made it out of the house without meeting her approval, they felt they could stand up to any other raised eyebrows.

Erika and Monika believe their experiences growing up made them "fashionably strong." As they continually embrace their unique points of view, which often include pieces they've created, they have seen firsthand what happens when they walk into a room and their essence says it all. "It's difficult to decide if people are staring at us because we have such great style, because we are twins, or because we are stylish twins," say Erika and Monika.

A BUSY WAY OF LIFE

With everything Erika and Monika are involved in, they lead a very busy life. "Juggling a lot of balls in the air is our way of life." The twins first realized they were jugglers in college. They were on the Western Wranglers dance team while choreographing the Gwendolyn Brooks dancers. "Oh, and we were full-time students who also participated in fashion shows and other extracurricular activities on campus as well." When they got stressed, their mom would encourage them to come home for a few days. They would refuse, and instead use that invitation as motivation to keep moving and to figure out how to manage it all. They knew they didn't want to quit.

Their day begins before 6 a.m., when they wake up and make breakfast smoothies. Then they speed walk at the lake. The rest of their day consists of working on the computer, attempting to reduce their to-do list, running errands, going to workout classes, checking the business mailbox and e-mails, dancing around with the baby, and crocheting.

FUN IN INSPIRATION

Erika and Monika are inspired by beautiful weather and the lake, which they visit often. "We're always looking at non-crochet pieces to figure out how to translate them into crochet," they say. When they lack inspiration, they get out of the house and go do activities with friends and family to relax. "Having fun is quite inspirational." The twins use many color palettes. "We tend to

Monika and Erika love to figure out more than one way to wear their designs, like their multi-way shawl, overhead sleeves, or fitted shrug. The twins are also open to layering and a variety of color palettes, depending on their mood.

78

① **②**

ERIKA & MONIKA'S PRIZED WEARABLES

- Double Stitch fitted shrug
- One-piece body suit from American Apparel
- Peep toe boots
- Fitted jackets with cinched waists
- Tube bras
- Double Stitch overhead sleeves

① Monika and Erika often add chunky, flamboyant jewelry pieces to their outfits, many of which they get from their jewelry designer friends. **②** The twins love textured pieces in their home, like this colorful knitted throw they're using as a table covering. **③** Monika and Erika enjoy wearing a variety of silhouettes, from tailored and angular to swingy with a lot of draping.

③

love bright colors and earthy tones equally," say Erika and Monika. "It's all a matter of the mood for the day."

The twins are always on the lookout for pieces, both for their wardrobe and their home, that will inspire them and show off their style. They both like to use unique items from resale shops, like jackets and dresses. They also love special belts with earthy elements, such as beads or wood. "Our collection of Double Stitch pieces are endless and varied as well. We both really love our remixes, like our T-shirts and skirts with crochet added for the trimming."

In their home, they are inspired by pieces that have a natural feel to them, or some sort of texture. "We find ourselves collecting braided baskets, patchwork and knitted throws, treasure chests with peeled-wood finishes, and pillows with fuzzy fabric," say Erika and Monika. "We like to feature things in the room that will add that certain pop." Whether it's through what they create or what they wear, there's no doubt that Erika and Monika have that certain pop down to an art.

SEXY REMIX HALTER TOP

This halter top incorporates **panels of cotton and denim** fabric with crochet. It **exudes** the **essence** of the Double Stitch **style** because their crochet styles have always been a merging of all of their different influences and interests.

WHAT YOU'LL NEED

Hand-dyed cotton fabric panels (3): 5½ x 30 inches (14 x 76.2 cm)

Denim fabric panels (2): 5½ x 30 inches (14 x 76.2 cm)

Large-eye needle

Acrylic worsted-weight yarn (Red Heart) in three coordinating pinks: one skein for the main halter section, stash yarn for the top accents and straps.

Crochet hook: Size I-9 (5.50 mm)

Hand needle

medium
4
Worsted, Afghan, Aran

1 Prepare the Panels

Cut two hand-dyed cotton fabric panels and two denim fabric panels that each measure 5½ x 30 inches (14 x 76.2 cm). Line them vertically and right sides up, alternating between the dyed cotton and denim. NOTE: The size of this garment may be altered by adding or reducing the number of panels and therefore modifying the number of top edge stitches and subsequent rows of crochet work.

2 Stitch the Panels Together

Thread a large-eye needle with Yarn A and join a denim panel to a dyed cotton panel by hand stitching together through the top edges: approximately 3½ inches (8.9 cm). Continue until all panels are joined to create the skirt portion. NOTE: Yarn A=halter; Yarn B=surface crochet; Yarn C=straps

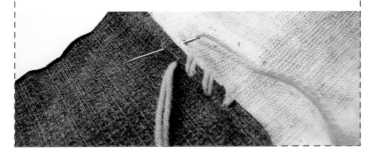

3 Stitch the Top Edge & Crochet

NOTE: ch=chain; sc=single crochet; dc=double crochet; rep=repeat; hdc=half double crochet.

Thread large-eye needle with Yarn A and create running stitch, about ½-inch (1.3 cm) wide, along the top edge of the joined panels. Row 1: from left to right, join Yarn A to first loop of the running stitch and chain 3 (counts as 1 dc), 2 dc in the same loop, *3 dc into each loop, rep from * across. Row 2: sc into each dc across. Rows 3–8: ch 2, sc into each sc across. Row 9: ch2, hdc into sc across. Rows 10–20: ch 2, hdc into each hdc across. Row 21: ch 2, hdc into each hdc across. Fasten off and weave in the end.

4 Surface Crochet

With Yarn B, pass the crochet hook through the stitch in the front of the top portion. Pull the yarn through the stitch, ch1, *pass the hook through the next stitch, pull the yarn through that stitch, pull the yarn through the 2 loops (single crochet), repeat * across. Fasten off and weave in the end of yarn. Repeat as desired.

5 Loop the Straps

With the project facing front, work from right to left and join Yarn C to the first hdc on the upper left corner of halter top. Ch 1 (counts as 1 sc), sc into the next 11 hdc, ch 80, sc into next 38 hdc across, ch 80, sc into remaining hdc. Fasten off and weave in the end of the yarn.

6 Add the Back Trim

With the project facing front and working along right edge from top to bottom, Row 1: Join Yarn A to upper right corner, ch2, hdc into each stitch across. Row 2: ch2, hdc into each hdc across, turn and create Right Side Eyelets as follows: Row 1: ch 2, hdc into next 4 hdc, *ch 1, skip next hdc, hdc into next 4 hdc, repeat from * across. Fasten off and weave in end. Repeat for left edge. Use Yarn A to chain 250 for corset tie.

7 Create the Cummerbund Belt

Cut cotton fabric into 5½ x 30 inches (14 x 76.2 cm) panel. Fold in half and stitch together with Yarn A. Use the needle and Yarn A to whipstitch the cummerbund to the waist. Cut excess cotton fabric from the cummberbund at either end, allowing the raw frayed ends to complement the raw and frayed look of the skirt panels.

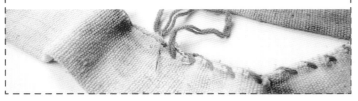

KAYTE TERRY

www.thisisloveforever.com

Kayte Terry manages several different creative passions by working full time in the Visual Department at Anthropologie's home office, writing books (including *Complete Embellishing* and *Appliqué Your Way*), designing and creating with colorful vintage fabrics, and operating her website. All the while, she keeps grounded and inspired by sticking to her personal style—a love of mixed-up patterns, color, and texture that is evident in both her wardrobe and her home.

MANAGING WHAT'S IMPORTANT

Kayte Terry often has way too much on her plate, and she says the key to managing it all is to get to the essence of what's most important to her. "When I went back to a full-time job, I knew that it was a job I really wanted to excel at," explains Kayte. "I knew that something else was going to have to go to make the job work." So she stopped selling at craft fairs and making things for her Etsy shop. Kayte admits it's now fun for her to just go to craft fairs as a shopper since she had never experienced that before.

Because she has so many things to remember, she keeps lots of lists. "I have one handwritten one that I carry everywhere, and then a task list that I keep on Gmail," shares Kayte. Plus there's the hope that she'll cross enough items off her lists to make time for two of her favorite activities—traveling the world with her husband and making a variety of handmade items for herself.

BACKWARD INSPIRATION

When Kayte is stumped for inspiration, she usually needs to clear her head and start over. She likes to get outside, take long walks, and just look around. "The typeface of a rusty old industrial sign, the neon shades of graffiti paint, the feeling of hope every spring when wildflowers and weeds poke through cracks in the sidewalk—these are the things that really get me going."

KAYTE'S PRIZED WEARABLES

- Vintage burgundy patchwork boots: "Totally beaten up, but in the best possible way."

- Gold necklace made by a friend that features a giant beetle encased in resin

- Her wedding band—a simple silver ring with the words "love forever" stamped on it

- Collection of bow-shaped brooches, some of which belonged to her late maternal grandmother: "I love to wear her jewelry."

- Headbands and hair fascinators with big flowers

- Black corduroy blazer with print flowers in autumnal colors

- Hand-printed dress made by a Brooklyn-based designer: "It ties right under the bust and the hem bubbles out into a big egg shape."

- Giant eyeglasses

❶ Kayte has a huge collection of vintage millinery supplies, ranging from more elegant roses to a silly trio of mushrooms on a bed of raffia. ❷ This bright red organizer allows Kayte to keep many of her supplies out in the open, which makes for easy access while creating. ❸ Vintage fabrics are one of Kayte Terry's favorite things, and she has a collection she uses in her various sewing projects. ❹ Headbands and hair fascinators with big flowers are part of Kayte's signature look.

Kayte likes to mix up interesting patterns and prints in her wardrobe, like the dress she's wearing here. Kayte tempers the bright colors of her chest of drawers and hanging illustrations with the more nuetral color of her walls.

people are wearing, but it's also important to not get too derivative." In other words, she likes to know what the trends are—but she doesn't always follow them.

Kayte has always felt she had a sense of style, though she admits some of her schoolmates might not agree. "When I was a kid, every day was a parade of costumes and crazy get-ups," says Kayte. "My grandparents had these amazing boxes and wardrobes in their attic that were just filled with old dresses and suits and costumes my mom and her sisters wore." And anything they couldn't find already in the attic? "We improvised," says Kayte. "My brother's Prince Charming outfit featured a cape made of an old bath towel fastened with one of my grandmother's sparkling brooches."

As Kayte grew up, she experimented with different fashions—from ripped punk fishnets to long, flowing hippie skirts. She recalls a particularly cathartic fashion moment: "It was when I deconstructed my junior high cheerleading outfit, adding safety pins and ripping up the plaid skirt," says Kayte. "It was one of my favorite high school outfits and one that said, 'I'm not a kid anymore.'"

Kayte looks to some of her favorite artists for inspiration, including Jean Shin, Eva Hesse, Louise Nevelson, Cézanne, Andy Goldsworthy, Ghada Amer, Patrick Dougherty, Simone Pheulpin, Megan Whitmarsh, Holly Farrell, and Tara Donovan. And in college? "I was totally obsessed with the movie *Unzipped*, a documentary about Isaac Mizrahi. Isaac talked about how his mom was such a style icon—one of her tricks was 'front to back'—she would wear clothes backward sometimes if she thought they looked better." That part of the movie has always stuck with Kayte, and she agrees that sometimes a shirt looks better worn backward.

Kayte attributes her current feelings about style to playing with costumes and fashion when she was growing up. Now, she thinks of style as something fun, something that can say who you are as much as who you aren't, and something that is far from frivolous.

FROM DRESS-UP TO STYLE SENSE

To Kayte, style is something that comes from within, and fashion is something that comes from the outside world. "I think it's really important to stay current with what's going on out there in the world and what

85

WOOD & ROSES NECKLACE

Kayte enjoys experimenting with sewing, so she thought it would be fun to create a necklace made from some of her **favorite fabrics and wooden beads**, which keep it from looking too "girly," says Kayte, plus they add a **natural element**.

WHAT YOU'LL NEED

Floral fabric strip: 1 x 60 inches (2.5 x 152.4 cm)

Stash fabric in coordinating colors and patterns

Tulle scraps

Thread in coordinating color

Hand needle

Wooden rings (3)

Wooden beads

1 Cut the Fabric

Cut a strip of fabric that measures 1 x 60 inches (2.5 x 152.4 cm). Cut strips of coordinating fabrics that measure 2 x 13 inches (5.1 x 33 cm) for the fabric flowers. Cut the tulle into similarly sized strips.

2 Press in Half

Press the long fabric strip for the necklace in half.

3 Press the Halves in Half

Press each half of the strip in half again.

4 Sew the Strip

Sew the folded strip down.

5 Cut & Sew Strip Pieces

Cut the sewn strip into three or four segments, as desired. Pin and hand sew each piece onto wooden circles. (NOTE: By having a wooden circle at one end of the necklace, you can loop the other end of the fabric necklace segment through the wooden circle to tie and secure the necklace when wearing it.)

6 Stitch the Flowers

Run the needle with thread through an edge of the flower fabric strip so that the strip can be scrunched into a circle.

(NOTE: You can add a layer of tulle to the fabric strips to add texture to a flower as desired.)

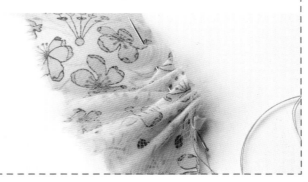

7 Finish the Flowers

Stitch the ends of the fabric flower together to finish.

8 Stitch Flowers to the Necklace

Use a needle and thread to add beads to the flower's center. Stitch the flower to the necklace. Repeat with the other fabric and tulle flowers.

MEGAN HUNT

Known to the world as **Princess Lasertron, Megan Hunt** is a bridal designer, blogger, and best friend. She is perhaps best known for her eclectic and whimsical bridal bouquets made of vintage buttons and felt, a true lasting heirloom piece. Megan also custom designs wedding gowns and hairpieces, in addition to DIY kits. She lives with her husband, David, and new baby, Alice, in Omaha, where she is heavily involved in the local art scene.

STYLE SAYS IT ALL

For Megan, style and fashion are not at all the same. "You can buy fashion. Fashion is not interesting," states Megan. "But when truly confident people, who are secure in their image and identity, walk into the room, it's entrancing." Megan believes that style is a result of respecting yourself, knowing who you want to be, and knowing how you want everyone in the world to see you—not from wanting to be someone else.

Personal style is something everyone should be actively working on, believes Megan. In fact, "Everyone owes it to themselves to define their personal style—it's no less necessary than any other personal maintenance," she says. She advises buying dramatic items that will become signature pieces. "First impressions do matter," she says, "and you do deserve to love how you look." When Megan sees someone with a strong sense of personal style walk into the room—whether that style is manifested through an interesting hairpiece or an eye-catching pair of shoes—she immediately notices. "I see that person and wonder who she is, what she's like, and what she does every day. And I think how exciting and full of creativity her life must be."

Megan's style has been shaped through the years in large part by her mother. It was her mother who made Megan feel free and safe in her room to try any outfit on before debuting it at school the next day. Growing up, Megan spent hours each week playing dress up in front of the mirror, experimenting with the mishmash of dresses, tights, sweaters, and accessories that found their way into her wardrobe. "Now as a designer, I see how my mother's openness to accepting my experiments in fashion correlate to her raising me to experiment in other venues of style and self-expression," she says.

89

THE ESSENCE OF MEGAN'S STYLE

- Respect: "Respect yourself and your style by only buying things that you can't live without."

- Risks: "Don't play it safe. Beautiful things are not necessarily perfect things."

- No limits: "Visualize yourself in an artistic vacuum. If you were never influenced by anyone else, if there was no one to impress, if there were no other artists or designers to make you feel inadequate, what could you create and wear?"

① Megan's young daughter, Alice, often accompanies her on various outings, from her daily errands to meetings at CAMP. **②** Megan lives with her husband and daughter in Omaha, where she enjoys meeting and working with local artists. **③** Megan's collection of brightly colored felt and thread is the beginning of her famous bouquets and headbands.

HARD WORK PAYS OFF

Megan's typical day starts between noon and 3 p.m. and ends at 7 or 8 a.m. as it feels most natural for her to work at night. When she wakes up, she reads her favorite blogs and answers e-mails, boxes up the things she made the night before for shipment, and interacts with her customers through Facebook, Twitter, and her website. She then gathers up her daughter, Alice, and goes to CAMP, the creative co-working facility she founded in downtown Omaha, where she works with several other self-employed designers and entrepreneurs throughout the day. "I also like to fit in some time every day to seek inspiration—whether it be online or outside in my beautiful city," says Megan. Afterward, her husband makes dinner and they catch up on their favorite TV shows while Megan works on sewing projects.

Megan is particularly busy in cycles, each lasting about four to five weeks. But she will never forget May of 2009—the month of 24 brides. "I do not know how I kept them all straight and got through the month. I think I slept about two hours a night." Megan got through that month knowing there was an end in sight. She knows she can push her body to meet the physical and emotional demands as long as she can

Megan loves to wear unique and hard-to-find pieces—like the great pairs of shoes she's modeling. The table Megan is decorating is in one of her favorite colors—yellow.

see the light at the end of the tunnel. "If you go 30 days without a weekend, I think you're entitled to a nice dinner and a few days off," she says. Plus, once the customers receive their orders, their feedback motivates Megan so much that she can't wait to get back to work.

MAKING HEADS TURN

Though Megan knows that style is so much more important than fashion, she still looks to fashion as a starting point for inspiration. She loves Alexander McQueen, Marc Jacobs, Tim Ford, and Betsey Johnson in particular. "My designer friend Steve Gordon says that when we're in a creative rut, the problem isn't lack of inspiration—it's lack of motivation," shares Megan. So when she feels like she's hit a block, she looks for motivation by talking to her creative friends and reading blogs and magazines. "Sometimes all I need to do is sit in a bookstore with a stack of magazines and a hot chocolate, and within ten minutes I'm itching to get out the door and back to the studio."

Megan also looks to certain people for inspiration, specifically when it comes to style. "I love Martha Stewart because she's very secure in her image and has created a lifestyle that really serves her aesthetic," she says. She also loves Lady Gaga for her eccentric glamour, as well as her friends. Megan has always noticed and been inspired by her mom, Mary Beth, who has the ability to express her style through decorating and home design. And her grandma, who likes to be called "Grand Catherine," is a true throwback to 1960s glamour and class, which is always inspiring to Megan.

Most of all, however, Megan is inspired by real people with true style walking around her city. "It's when you have the confidence to dress like 'you' and not 'them' that really makes heads turn."

RUFFLED FLOWER BRACELET

Here Megan shows how to make the **basic structure** of her famous bracelets so **anyone** can **embellish** it to suit their **own style**.

WHAT YOU'LL NEED

Blue wool felt strip: 1½ x 30 inches (3.8 x 76.2 cm)

Green wool felt strip: ½ x 11 inches (1.3 x 27.9 cm)

Pink wool felt panel: 8 x 10 inches (20.3 x 25.4 cm)

Hand needle

Embroidery floss in coordinating colors

Black marker

Cardboard

Button

Hook-and-eye fasteners (2 pairs)

Sewing thread in coordinating color

1 Form the Ruffles

Begin forming ruffles on a 1½ x 30-inch (3.8 x 76.2 cm) strip of felt by holding up a 1-inch (2.5 cm) section of felt every 2 inches (5.1 cm). Stitch in place by hand sewing down the center of the strip as you ruffle it.

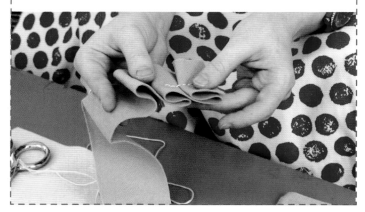

2 Add Dimension

Layer a ½-inch (1.3 cm) strip of felt down the center of the ruffled piece to add some dimension. Stitch into place.

3 Draw a Petal Shape

Hand draw a petal shape onto cardboard and cut it out. On the large sheet of felt, trace the petal shape 20 times and cut them all out.

5 Gather & Fluff the Petals

Tie the two ends of the embroidery floss together, gathering the petals in the process. Gently fluff the petals from the center of the flower to create a nice fluffy peony shape.

4 Create the Flower

Thread a needle with a 20-inch (50.8 cm) strand of embroidery floss. Create the flower by sewing a running stitch along the bottom of each petal, leaving the ends free. You'll end up with a long strand of petal shapes.

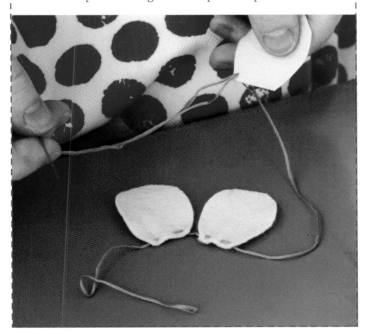

6 Add the Flower

Center the flower on the ruffled strip of felt, which is the bracelet base. Secure the flower and add the buttons in one step by sewing through the bracelet base, through the center of the flower, through the button holes, and back down through the bracelet base. Holding the bracelet around your wrist, measure where to place two pairs of hook-and-eye fasteners for the closure. Sew into place with sewing thread.

SONYA NIMRI

Sonya Nimri is a designer who creates—or re-creates—everything from jewelry to home décor and from clothing to celebrations. Her love for color and energy, coupled with inner elegance and panache, have guided Sonya through years of experience in creating beautiful living spaces. In her career as an artist, Sonya has repurposed clothing, arranged flowers, dressed up a home, decorated cakes, painted, sculpted, and knitted—and she has done it all on a very public stage with several TV appearances to her credit. Though her artistic mediums have varied over the years, Sonya's sense of style has remained consistent, a tribute to her as an artist and an individual.

A PRACTICAL YET ELEGANT STYLE

Sonya grew up in the '90s. While she has always felt she had style, she says it can be a little difficult to look at pictures of herself in middle school. "It wasn't until I lived in Belgium, when I was 16, that the pragmatism of my thrifty household and the elegance of European design began to coalesce into something I could call my own." That special talent for repurposing and her eye for design have shaped her style to this day.

Sonya sees style as something she creates—something more individual, more personal, than fashion. Style is more courageous for her, especially when her style rejects the fashion of the day. "I admire the style of my husband and two-year-old son, because they're fearless in their selection and will wear anything, anytime." Sonya doesn't pay much attention to how people react to what she's wearing; instead, she trusts the instinct that drives her look.

Sonya is instinctively all about colors and layers. In fact, when she dresses, she likes to think of herself as a dessert. For example, one day she might feel like spumoni—she'll wear green or brown, with white and touches of pink. Another day she might feel like chocolate raspberry cake, with various shades of brown and traces of raspberry. Another day? A big banana split, with white, brown, and red layers. "I think layering colors like that has a subliminal effect on people, making them happy," says Sonya. "Yummy."

95

① Sonya can't live without French macarons—they are delectable and come in some of her favorite colors. ② Nature inspires Sonya, so bringing a bit of the outdoors into her home in the form of flowers and a beloved horse statue creates inspiration every day. ③ Sonya's son has no fear when it comes to his style, something that continually inspires Sonya.

THE ESSENCE OF SONYA'S STYLE

- Layers, layers, layers: patterned tights over solid ones under a simple skirt makes for a good start
- An item that she's received as a gift: to remind her that she's loved
- Nothing with words, but rather clothes that speak for themselves
- Cotton or cashmere scarves: a must to keep the chest warm
- At least one item that she's made

Sonya's favorite color palette is decidedly jewel tones tempered by neutrals. "Hot pink with olive green, or beige and tangerine, for example. Love it," she says.

WIDE-EYED FOR INSPIRATION

One of Sonya's obsessions? Taxidermy. "Don't know where that came from," she says, "but something about the captured moment, and the kind of gray area between art and science, ornament and artifact, really appeals to me." Her house is full of antlers, and even a stuffed goose named Vladmir. Though she's passionate about taxidermy, she likes

Sonya can't live without orchids in her house. Here, she sits next to a group of them wearing a dress in her favorite color palette—jewel tones.

to take the hunting-library element out of it by softening the whole effect with orchids, patterns, and fun decoupage portraits of the family. In addition to her taxidermy collection, Sonya treasures her box full of vintage buttons. She loves to sift through the buttons made from old ivory, leather, and bamboo for inspiration because it really "brings her to another era."

Sonya draws inspiration from, literally, everywhere. "I'm a wide-eyed sort of person," she says. Sonya loves the world around her, and is constantly absorbing new elements where she encounters them, especially in nature and relationships. If she's not feeling inspired, she takes a break from it all by doing something else. Whether it's cooking, cleaning, or taking a bike ride, she has realized that getting stressed about a project certainly doesn't help. "After all, my work is meant to inspire joy," explains Sonya. "If I'm not happy creating it, then people won't be happy making it." She doesn't push it, and crafts only when it's fun for her to do so, which, judging by her ever-growing résumé of fabulous projects, is pretty often.

Some of Sonya's trademark projects breathe new life into outcast materials. For example, she likes to work vintage scarves into her repurposed sweaters. She uses the fabric as the sleeves, trim for the collar, and leather from skirts or purses for the elbow patches. She also creates little purses out of the actual neck of turtleneck sweaters.

97

1 Sonya is known for breathing new life into outcast garments; many times she uses scrap fabric to create a patch in a fun shape to cover up holes. **2** Part of Sonya's small collection of antique brooches resides on these mannequins. **3** Sonya doesn't need her shoes to always be name brands—instead, she'd rather have them speak for themselves.

SONYA'S PRIZED WEARABLES

- Hot pink pashmina scarf from Nepal: she's had it for 10 years and wears it at least twice a week

- Mike and Chris burgundy leather jacket

- Vintage button headband

- 1930s star sapphire engagement ring

- Brown work boots

- Knee-high tie-dye cotton socks (that no one is supposed to know she's wearing underneath her work boots)

DOMESTIC DIVA

A few years ago, Sonya simultaneously had a full-time office job, traveled as a spokesperson for Michaels (doing early morning TV shows and the like), and wrote her first book. "I never thought it could get more intense than that...and then I had a baby. That's pretty all-encompassing," she says. Now, she can't imagine having two or more little ones—but she can't wait, either. After all, Sonya credits her own mom and dad with helping her become who she is today.

Her days now are full of caring for and playing with her young son, teaching Mommy and Me craft classes at the UCLA Family Commons, and crafting and blogging in her spare minutes. And what's next for Sonya? Well, one thing she'd like to try is taxidermy, so she can create her own version of her favorite home décor. In the jewelry world, she wants to experiment with soldering and lost-wax casting, and she'd also like to learn to cut precious gemstones. But whatever she creates, one thing's for sure—this domestic diva has a style, presence, and confidence all her own.

SONYA CAN'T LIVE WITHOUT

- Orchids in her house
- French macarons
- The movie *Funny Face*
- Mariage-Frères Bolero Tea
- C.A. Stefani Aqua di Rosa (as a facial mister)

Sonya appreciates anything that brings her to another era, including vintage tins that she uses to organize her desk. Quirky art pieces, like this medieval-themed shadow box, inspire Sonya with their stories and colors.

99

BRILLIANTLY BUTTONED UPCYCLED SWEATER

Sonya has been repurposing clothes by adding a **colorful flair** for most of her life. Here, she explains how to create one of her signature projects, the **cardigan**, which she loves because of its **versatility**—it provides **warmth**, yet allows ventilation if she gets **toasty**.

WHAT YOU'LL NEED

Wool sweater

Silk chiffon panels (2):
11 x 35 inches (27.9 x 88.9 cm)

Velvet strip: 4 x 34 inches (10.2 x 86.4 cm)

Thread in coordinating color

Faux fur strip: 24 inches long (61 cm)

Fabric glue

Hand needle

Large snap & assorted buttons

1 Cut an Old Sweater

Take an old wool sweater and cut the arms and along the bottom to a length that you desire. Make a cut at the front center point of the sweater and also cut out a neckline into a shape that you like. (This sweater started out as a turtleneck. The neckline was cut in a large rectangular manner, allowing the top portions to naturally drape down to create collars.) Zigzag stitch the raw edges.

2 Measure for Additions

Measure the circumference of the cut armhole and multiply by three to calculate the length of a piece of silk that you will cut into a rectangle. For this sweater, the armhole was 11 inches (27.9 cm) around so the silk was 33 inches (83.8 cm) in length. The width of the silk can be up to you. For this project, the width was 11 inches (27.9 cm).

3 Prepare the Silk

With right sides together, fold the silk lengthwise in half, pin, and sew on both of the short ends. Turn right side out and then add a running stitch at the top edge and pull the ends to gather the silk.

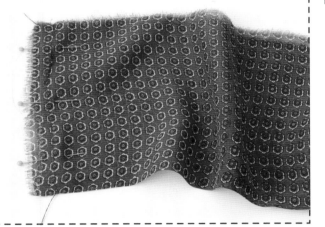

4 Attach the Silk

Pin the gathered silk to the inside of the sweater's armhole and sew in place. This will allow the silk to drape on the arm with a nice little opening.

5 Gather & Sew the Velvet

Gather a strip of velvet that you cut, pin, and sew in the same fashion as the silk. Sew this velvet onto the neckline.

6 Add the Faux Fur

Gather a piece of faux fur and use fabric glue to it attach on top of the velvet.

7 Embellish with Buttons

Hand sew a large snap at the center of the center front opening. Finish by sewing on decorative buttons.

MEGAN NICOLAY

Megan Nicolay is an obsessive DIY-er with a love for refashioning everyday items, most notably the T-shirt. This desire to rethink and repurpose what she already owns is a trait that carries through from her work on her website, as well as her books, *Generation T: 108 Ways to Transform a T-shirt* and *Generation T: Beyond Fashion: 120 Ways to Transform a T-shirt*. Living in New York City, Megan is always on the lookout for the next T-shirt she can slash.

A FAST-PACED ONE-WOMAN SHOW

Megan wears many hats. Currently, she works by day as a book editor, specializing in DIY and craft titles. At night and on weekends, she writes, illustrates, designs, and makes projects for her books and her blog. "I don't sleep a lot," says Megan, "but I also love the pace—I'm most productive when I'm busy. The momentum keeps me going." Though she does entice her friends with dessert and home-cooked meals when she needs help finishing samples, there isn't an around-the-clock (or even part-time) team behind the scenes. "I smile a little when I see posts online like, 'I can't believe the people at Generation T got back to me,' because yes, those 'people' would be me," Megan says.

When Megan was working on her first book, she was writing, making projects, illustrating, working a day job, sharing an apartment with three roommates, and carrying on a long-distance relationship with her now husband. "It was hard," says Megan, "but I managed it on very little sleep and with a lot of patience and support from those around me." When Megan has a chance for some free time, she loves to read, play in the park, go to shows, make things, snuggle with her husband and her cat, problem-solve, bake, run, or make a grilled cheese sandwich. "I make a mean grilled cheese sandwich," says Megan. "Really, I think I've perfected it."

PLAYING DRESS UP

Megan's mom and dad always thought she made some "pretty fly" style choices when she was little—"no matter how many cringe-worthy photos exist that document otherwise," says Megan. She has photos of herself and her sister Sophie wearing leotards, scarves, mismatched shoes, and Mardi Gras beads, with about 40 plastic animal-shaped barrettes in their hair. "And the delightful thing is we weren't playing dress up," says Megan. "That was just how we liked to dress."

THE ESSENCE OF MEGAN'S STYLE

- Fun: Including mixing whimsy with work-appropriate office wear. "I'll work in plastic accent jewelry with my sterling silver, or edgy T-shirts with more refined skirt silhouettes."

- Statement piece. Statement piece. Statement piece.

- Outfits that mix decades: For example, she'll pair vintage cowboy boots with a skirt she bought last week at Forever 21, then add a T-shirt she picked up at a thrift store during "summer road trip 1999"—which she refashioned in the summer of 2000 when she was living in New York City—and top it all off with an antique brooch from the 1940s that she turned into a hair clip.

- Outfits that create contradictions: "If an outfit's too rough around the edges, I'll wear a delicate piece of jewelry to soften it up."

She fell for the standard trends in middle school: the pegged pants; slouch socks; scrunchies; and pleats. But she also grew up wearing clothes that her mom made, so she learned at a very young age to appreciate one-of-a-kind pieces. "Or two-of-a-kind," says Megan, "since my mom indulged my desires to match my dolls and made the dress or skirt in miniature."

Today, Megan still likes to play dress up and put crazy things in her hair. "If anything, my style has become more urban," says Megan. She grew up surrounded by trees, lakes, and mountains in a very small town in upstate New Hampshire. That aesthetic—which Megan deems a little bit country—has definitely shaped and mixed with the more sidewalk-to-skyscraper landscape and influences of her Brooklyn home—which Megan calls a bit rock n' roll. "I'm influenced by the people around me, characters in literature, even strangers on the street. I don't think my style reflects any particular decade or genre, nor do I think I'm particularly on trend. I wear what I like."

❶ Megan's cat is named Tulu—she is often at hand to witness Megan's creativity. ❷ Vintage purses line the shelves in Megan's closet, as she's always on the lookout for bright and unique accessories.

Megan organizes everything by color, both in her home closet and in her studio. That way she can always find the exact color she's in the mood for.

EVER-CHANGING CREATIVE PROCESS

To jumpstart her creative process, Megan might take a walk or sit and people-watch. She might have a conversation with a friend or sibling, hit shuffle and see what music comes on, or consult her sketchbook to see if any recent notes or observations inspire her. She also likes to take things apart and put them back together again to see how they're constructed—a self-declared tinkerer.

Megan keeps the inspiration flowing by shifting between tasks. "Part of what kept me moving forward on my book projects was that I was able to engage so many parts of my brain," she says, as she did when alternating between writing step-by-step instructions and project introductions, illustrating, cutting, and sewing. "Sometimes I simply need to switch it up, which encourages a solo game of musical chairs as I move from desk to light box to chair to floor to sewing machine to couch to computer and back again."

Megan is also inspired on a personal and a professional level by her parents, who are both artists. Her mom's a photographer who dabbles in handmade fleece wearables, and her dad's a photographer, mixed-media artist, former potter, and high school and college art teacher. "As parents, they supported my developing interests with such enthusiasm," says Megan. "Today, I still turn to my parents for creative advice. The difference is that it's more reciprocal now. Some kids find their path by rebelling; I followed my parents' example, and I'm so grateful for the example they set." With such a history of creativity and family support, it's no wonder that Megan is able to be the creative force and innovative crafter she is.

"PICK ME" ROSETTE BIB NECKLACE

The **yo-yo** is a traditional quilting technique that Megan likes to call **rosettes**. She loves how the rosettes can be incorporated in a number of ways into so many different projects.

WHAT YOU'LL NEED

T-shirt

Hand needle

Thread in coordinating color

 1 Cut the Circles

Find an old T-shirt that you'd like to reuse. Cut one circle about 3 inches (7.6 cm) in diameter, and then use it to make about 15 more circles of the same size. The sleeve section is a great place to cut from.

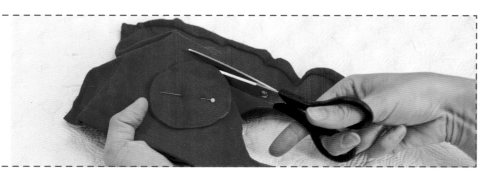

2 Cut a Strip

From the same T-shirt, cut a strip that measures ¼ x 12 inches (.6 x 30.5 cm) to use later as the back of the necklace. Stretch it into a cord and cut it in half.

3 Sew the Circles

Begin a simple running stitch around the outside edge of one circle.

4 Gather to Create Rosette

When you finish sewing around the circle, pull the thread to gather it. Tie the ends off and flatten the center to create the rosette.

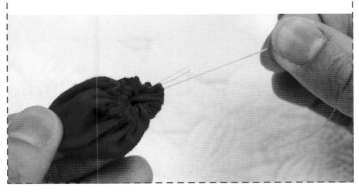

5 Connect the Rosettes

Once you have several rosettes completed, press two and sew them along one edge.

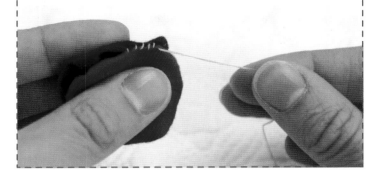

6 Continue Adding Rosettes

Add more rosettes until you are pleased with the shape and arrangement of the bib portion of the necklace.

7 Finish the Necklace

Sew the strips from step 2 onto each side of the bib portion, to complete the back of the necklace.

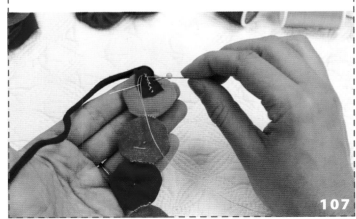

107

RUTH SINGER

www.ruthsinger.com
www.mantua-maker.blogspot.com

Ruth Singer's exceptional textile artwork uses innovative variations of quilting, pleating, and gathering to create unusual textures and effects—all of which are shown in her books, *Sew It Up* (published as *The Sewing Bible* in the United States) and *Sew Eco*. Ruth also teaches textile techniques and history through workshops and at various museums.

FLEXIBLE & FULFILLING DAYS

No two days are ever the same for Ruth since she works freelance and has no fixed pattern of work. "As often as possible I am in the studio, working on new designs or writing, but all too often I seem to be doing administration and organizing my teaching schedule." Teaching takes up much of Ruth's time, but she loves it. She also works with galleries, art organizations, and community groups. She is usually going somewhere different every week, which is always fun for her.

Ruth spends time each day online, reading blogs, chatting on Twitter, and keeping an eye on the craft and textile world. "I also feel something is wrong if I haven't picked up my knitting for at least 30 minutes or so each day, usually accompanied by BBC Radio 4, which is a serious addiction." When Ruth isn't working, she loves to walk and ride her bike around her city of Leicester. She enjoys the woods and green fields that are close to her home. Ruth loves food and cooking and she especially likes that her community has good, readily available Indian food.

When Ruth was writing her book, *Sew it Up* (published as *The Sewing Bible* in the United States), it was the busiest time she'd ever had. She wrote the book in about six months, from starting the projects to finalizing the text. At that same time, she was working on a freelance project, to create teaching resources for contemporary art. "I actually forgot how to relax," says Ruth. "But I managed by being very organized with the work, setting myself schedules to finish different small chunks. I also employed several people to help with various bits of the work."

109

1 Ruth owns textiles from all over the world, many of which she hangs or displays directly on the wall. **2** She collects contemporary art pieces, like ceramics from Katrin Moye and paper artwork by Jennifer Collier and Iain Perry. **3** Ruth's love of historic textiles carries over to buttons as well, which she uses in many of her textile projects.

how people actually lived 500 years ago." Ruth received a master's degree in Museum Studies—she wanted to be a curator and dreamed of working in a costume museum looking after old clothes (her idea of heaven). She spent ten years working in museums before she realized she wanted to set out on her own. Now, she keeps up her freelance work in museums while also working with textiles.

Ruth says that the main reason she became a textile artist was her love of historic textiles, which continue to be an inspiration to her today—she loves the texture and techniques found in old clothing and textiles. "Because I worked in museums, for years I had access to wonderful stuff—mostly 19th-century garments—and they always gave me ideas," says Ruth. She learned how ancient textiles, such as tablet weaving, were created, and she credits her current desire to make innovative textiles to those lessons.

In recent years, Ruth's work has been inspired by 18th- and 19th-century dress trimmings, particularly pleating and gathering, as well as old and traditional sewing

INSPIRED BY HISTORIC TEXTILES

Ruth received her BA in Medieval Studies, where she focused on Art History and Palaeography (the study of old handwriting)—which is interesting, considering her current career in textiles. "I loved my degree and liked nothing better than reading medieval English wills and letters to find out

RUTH'S PRIZED WEARABLES

- Zebra dress, a super-simple smock dress made from Echino quilting fabric in purples and turquoise: "It's not subtle, or even elegant, but it's quirky and silly and I love it."
- Two dresses made from the same Vogue pattern, a smock style—one in gray wool and one in vintage '50s green and brown silk
- 1950s ribbed silk black coat: "It makes me feel utterly glamorous, but I hardly ever wear it as it is so impractical in my life at the moment."
- Rob Ryan for Clothkits skirt she made with a personalized quilted and scalloped hem
- Collection of assorted aprons, both handmade and vintage
- Red Clarks shoes
- Purple wool dress

Ruth loves collecting vintage handbags, which she uses on her outings to various vintage shops and art exhibitions. This green and brown silk smock-style dress is one of Ruth's favorites. She hoarded the fabric for ages before she finally realized it was meant to be this piece.

techniques like Suffolk puffs (the British name for yo-yos). "I like to play around, experiment with fabrics, and create new and original variations on the techniques," says Ruth. She is often inspired by the materials she works with—sometimes a piece of vintage velvet or silk will tell her just what it wants to be.

FABULOUS & SECONDHAND

Ruth's love of old clothes has carried over into her personal wardrobe. This, combined with the desire to have her own fabulous wardrobe, inspired her to start making clothes as a teenager. Today, most of her clothes are bought secondhand, at either charity shops or vintage shops, or made by her. "I wish I had time to make all the clothes I want to," says Ruth, "but for now, I have plenty in my wardrobe that I have collected over the last ten years or so."

Ruth tends to wear skirts most of the time, although she says trousers are often necessary for cycling in the windy British climate. Ruth doesn't wear jeans, trainers, or suits, but instead gravitates toward loose-fitting dresses and smock tops. "I like to mix and clash bright colors, striped tights, colored shoes, and lots of layers," she says. Ruth also has a good selection of coats and wool socks, scarves, hats, and gloves about for dealing with cold temperatures. She usually only wears earrings and brooches, but she has a jewelry box full of handmade items she picked up in India or Mexico or locally, plus a few vintage pieces and a few textile jewelry pieces that she has made herself.

Most importantly, Ruth doesn't like to buy anything new. Whether it's sewing projects using recycled fabric, or buying a fabulous wardrobe addition at a second-hand shop, she looks to the quirky and the unique for inspiration in all facets of her life.

111

Ruth Singer is **passionate** about creating **unusual textures** and **sculptural effects** with fabric. This scarf contains elegant gathers that are **cleverly constructed** using techniques that are reflective of Ruth's passion.

WHAT YOU'LL NEED

Outer scarf fabric (lavender Dupioni silk):
9½ x 55 inches (24.1 x 139.7 cm)

Lining fabric (cream Dupioni silk):
9½ x 55 inches (24.1 x 139.7 cm)

Materials to create circle template

Fabric-marking tool

Thread in coordinating color

Knitting needle (or other sharp object)

Hand needle

ELEGANT GATHERED SCARF

1 Cut Fabric & Create Circle Template

Cut two pieces of fabric—one for the outer scarf and one for the lining so that each measures 55 x 9½ inches (139.7 x 24.1 cm). Place right sides together and pin along edges. Create a circle template with a 6½-inch (16.5 cm) diameter and draw a series of partial circles on the edges of the scarf, for a total of six, spaced randomly along both edges of the scarf.

2 Stitch & Pivot

Sew small stitches along the straight edges using a ⅝-inch (1.6 cm) seam allowance. When you reach the circles, pivot the needle in the fabric and sew carefully along the marked line. Leave one section (about six inches [15.2 cm]) of straight edge open.

3 Trim & Turn

Trim the seam allowances in the circles to ¼ inch (.6 cm).
Trim the straight edge seam allowances to ½ inch (1.3 cm).
Turn the scarf right side out using the opening.

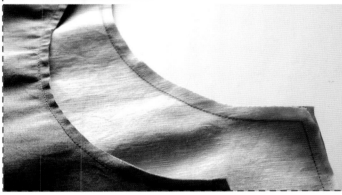

5 Add Large Running Stitches

Press all the edges, but don't worry too much if the circles
are crinkly. Sew up the opening using small hand stitches.
Sew along the circular edges using a double thread and large
running stitches, ¾ inch (1.9 cm) from the edge.

4 Push Out the Corners

Use a knitting needle to push out all the corners so
the scarf will lie flat.

6 Create the Gathers

Pull up the thread to create gathers and fasten the thread
with several tiny stitches. Repeat with all of the circles.

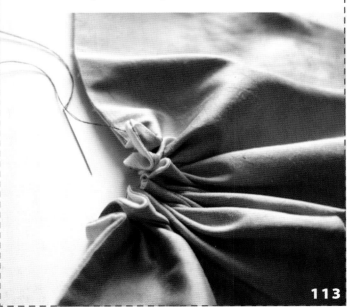

SANDY STONE

www.sandystonedesignstudio.com

As a creator of unique upholstery pieces and items for the home, **Sandy Stone's** style transcends both home and wardrobe. Whether it's bright colors and fun fabrics, or a neutral palette and textured materials, Sandy has a look that's all her own—and a talent that's unbeatable.

CUSTOM WORK & BUSY TIMES

Sandy always begins the day with morning coffee and the newspaper. Some of her days are spent working on commissioned projects, including slipcovers, simple upholstery, pillows, or cushions—created in styles ranging from straightforward to expressively free-reign.

When Sandy has a free moment in her day, she loves hunting for vintage goods and unusual useful junk. "A trip to the flea market with my girlfriends is my idea of a great time," she says. Styling her wares in her booth at Hunt & Gather, a local shop, is a different kind of creative outlet that she also enjoys. "If I spend too much time behind my sewing machine I get crabby and stiff," says Sandy.

Sandy recently finished what she says was the busiest year of her life. "In my spare time, I created 30-some projects for a how-to book, *Fabric Remix*, which I also wrote and illustrated," says Sandy. "I had to cut down on my custom work during that period in order to manage the stress." And how does Sandy make it through her stressful times? "Long walks and yoga," she says. "And wine."

PERSONAL UPHOLSTERY & VINTAGE NOTIONS

If anyone were to walk into Sandy's house, they would probably take a seat in one of the many chairs that fill her living area. "It's often filled with a combination of 'before' and 'after' chairs and sofas, and I'm often sitting in one of the 'afters,'" she says. Many of her furnishings have an industrial feel to them: for example, she made her coffee table by adding giant casters to an old barn gate.

115

1 Sandy collects wire baskets and bins to hold her vintage fabrics and found textiles. **2** This is the upstairs studio where Sandy spends much of her day working on both her own projects and commissioned projects. **3** The coffee carafes shown here hold all of Sandy's vintage sewing notions, including buttons, buckles, trims, and measuring tapes. **4** Sandy has to set aside at least a few days a week to experiment with new ideas, many of which she records in the notebooks she keeps in her studio.

THE ESSENCE OF SANDY'S STYLE

- Comfort
- Affordability
- Machine washability
- Neutral colors
- Closely fitted pieces
- Dresses that are above the knee, with an empire waist
- Shoes that are comfortable, yet give her some height, like Dansko clogs or those with a platform heel
- A dash of funk, or a little vintage wear to make the outfit unique: "For example, I'll strip a cardigan of its buttons and replace them with mismatched vintage buttons, or use a narrow vintage necktie as a belt."
- A cute haircut: "It's a no-fail way to add immediate style."

Sandy loves hunting for vintage fabrics because she prefers using reclaimed materials in her creations. She lets her work evolve by constantly reusing and altering with fabrics like these.

don't have to think much about it." As far as particular favorites go, she has quite a few V-neck Mossimo knit tops from Target—a staple for her.

INSPIRED BY RAW MATERIALS & CLOSE FAMILY

Most of the materials used in Sandy's work are reclaimed items. "I spend a few days each month scavenging for raw materials at estate sales and thrift shops," she says. "The raw materials that I find and bring home are what inspire me." Her husband and her mother also serve as inspiration to Sandy. When she first met her husband, who is an architect, he introduced her to thoughtful design, which inspired her to go to art school. "His influence was huge in terms of helping me discover the 'artist' in me," says Sandy. Her mother, the ultimate DIY-er, also unknowingly passed down her creativity through her thrifty, practical ways.

Sandy goes through phases as to which colors inspire her. "Presently I find myself working with and being inspired by neutrals and highly textured materials, especially after a long period of working with saturated color and mixing wild prints." Sandy doesn't stick with one look for very long, and likes to challenge herself to change things up. This challenge is perhaps what's made her aesthetically pleasing upholstery pieces so charming—with an ever-present need for change, Sandy is able to hold true to her style, while creating pieces that are one of a kind.

Sandy's studio walls are completely covered with vintage scarves. "I just love them, but I feel too self-conscious wearing them, so this is how I have them in my life," she says. She loves metal zippers, and often uses them in her work as decorative elements in addition to their functional purpose.

CASUAL & FUNKY STYLE

Sandy greatly admires the style of her two grown daughters. "Both of them have always had a sassy, individual way of putting their own look together." As for her own style, Sandy's work is very physical and often very messy, so her wardrobe consists mainly of basic casual wear. "If you were to walk into my house on any given day," she says, "you would probably see me wearing a very tattered pair of cut-offs and a T-shirt, or jeans and a long-sleeve V-neck in the winter."

Sandy loves that her wardrobe is so small that it needs no organization. "I love how simple it is," she says. "Everything fits in one small closet, and I

FUNKY & UPHOLSTERED SKIRT

Since Sandy is an **upholsterer** and a textile artist, her work, which she calls pretty funky, **centers on textiles**. This simple black skirt that she purchased at a thrift store is **instantly personalized** with different-sized columns of upholstery samples.

WHAT YOU'LL NEED

Upholstery sample strips in assorted sizes

Black skirt

Thread in coordinating color

1 Gather Upholstery Samples

Collect some upholstery or drapery samples. Check out local upholstery supply shops or furniture stores for discontinued samples, which are usually just thrown out.

2 Find a Skirt

Pull a solid-colored skirt from your closet, or purchase one.

3 Cut Rectangles from Fabrics

From the upholstery or drapery samples, choose several pieces that look fun together and cut them into different-sized rectangles.

4 Create a Fringe

Pull the loose threads along all four raw edges to create a fringe for added interest.

5 Arrange Upholstery on Skirt

Arrange the rectangles along the hemline of the skirt, front and back, in a way that pleases you. Pin them in place.

6 Sew Samples to Skirt

Machine stitch the samples into place, removing the pins as you go.

Alternative Option

Consider adding upholstery or drapery samples to tattered and worn-out denim shorts or jeans.

BONZIE
& GER

With tattered ruffles and an old-world appeal, **Bonzie** and **Ger** have a style all their own. They impart that style on skirts, cuffs, corsages, jackets, and corsets that they sell to clients all over the world—providing the perfect outfit or accessory for what is often a big day or special occasion. Their business keeps their days full, but they both work well under pressure. They take on all the roles required of a creative business owner, while exuding poise and self-confidence in their romantic style.

CONFIDENCE IN THEIR INTRIGUING STYLE

Bonzie and her business partner Ger have always been quite brave when it comes to their personal approach to style. "It's about choosing a look and owning it afterward," says Bonzie. "I was always a courageous dresser in my youth, and I often heard pals saying, 'Oh I wish I were brave enough to wear that,' so I guess experimenting with different looks and putting things together creatively was a way of dressing from a young age." Bonzie thinks that willingness to explore different ways of dressing and taking a more quirky approach has given her and Ger the confidence to put out a style that, though it isn't the current *en trend* brand, is quickly becoming recognized for its characteristic edginess.

Today, Bonzie and Ger approach their personal styles in a professional way. "It's our hope that folks see our style as an extension of our business, and that upon walking into a room they'll notice something a little special about our appearance that will leave them wondering and intrigued about what we do for a living," shares Bonzie. Bonzie and Ger have often turned up at a meeting and introduced themselves as Bonzie and Ger from Bonzie Designs. On a few occasions, the person they're meeting responds, "I already figured that." Bonzie and Ger say that is wonderful to hear; they are glad that they emit a quirkiness that people respond positively to.

1 Regal yellow is a color often seen in Bonzie's work, right alongside various antique embellishments often seen on their combined work. **2** Tattered ruffles of tulle are incorporated in many of their pieces. **3** Deep teals and rich jewel shades are among Bonzie's favorite color palette—the jewel tones help break up the muted and antiquated shades they are known for.

THE ESSENCE OF BONZIE & GER'S STYLE

- A muted color palette, including grays, blacks, creams, and olive green

- Something with a litte ruffle and romance

- Flattering cuts

- One statement piece of jewelry: Bonzie's clothes often have textures and interesting details. Several pieces of layered jewelry would be too busy, but she does like one statement or chunky piece.

- Wearable art as opposed to fancy commercial work

MANAGING THEIR MANY HATS

To begin each morning, Bonzie takes her laptop into bed with her ("Irish mornings are cold," she explains). She answers the correspondence that has come during the night from clients all over the world, and then squeezes in domestic duties, breakfast, and a run on the treadmill before she washes up and dresses for the day. She then sits down at the sewing machine to sew and create until lunchtime (with a coffee break in between). Bonzie and Ger tend to incoming e-mails, blog postings, and Facebook throughout the day as well. The last part of the day is packaging and posting to meet their daily deadline of 4:30 p.m. for the

Bonzie and Ger both love the escapism that they are able to find in books and movies, as well as the chance to clear the mind and get distracted for the duration of the film or story.

post office. They then prep for the following day by gathering fabric, cutting out patterns, or updating their online social networks. "At this point of the night, I like to have the TV on in the background and feel like I'm starting to relax from work a little," says Bonzie, "but I only keep one eye on the TV and another on the laptop. I guess one could say we are rarely not working. It's a full-time career."

"Running your own business can be incredibly taxing at times," admits Bonzie. "Much of the strain comes from wearing so many hats, and not in the literal sense. Some days it's an adrenaline rush reaching deadlines, overcoming challenges, and facing new opportunities head on. However, there are days when it can get a little overwhelming, especially if personal challenges are pulling on our focus." In order to manage everything, Bonzie and Ger employ a triage system for prioritizing their to-do list in order of importance, as well as time management—with customer orders being first on the list.

LETTING IN INSPIRATION

The musical group Evanescence provides instant inspiration for Bonzie with their provoking,

haunting, passionate, and chilling music. "Their music opens up the creativity in me and helps take my mind away from normal personal life," Bonzie shares. Though music is one of her sources for inspiration, Bonzie finds inspiration in all corners of life. "Really it's not so much about looking for inspiration as it is about being open to inspiration and letting it in," says Bonzie. And when she hits that dreaded creative block? "This is a pretty sad state of affairs for an artist," admits Bonzie. When it hits, she distracts herself with less creative aspects of the business, like accounting or stocking. Normally by the time she's completed one of those tasks, Bonzie is grateful for anything creative she can get her hands on.

Whether it's singer Imogen Heap's unapologetic sense of style, Daphne Guinness' edginess in everyday clothing, or Vivienne Westwood's ability to make the odd in fashion look couture, Bonzie looks for inspiration everywhere—in the fashion world, on the Internet, and in her own personal life. And all of that inspiration, creativity, and hard work can only lead to better things for Bonzie and Ger—including a longstanding dream to own a boutique of their very own in Ireland.

TATTERED COUTURE CUFF

This cuff features **frayed lace**, vintage accoutrements, and romantic **tattered** fabric that are all signature elements of Bonzie Designs.

WHAT YOU'LL NEED

Base fabric (neutral cotton): 3 x 7 inches (7.6 x 17.8 cm)

Batting: slightly larger than base fabric

Lining fabric (neutral loose-weave cotton): 3 x 7 inches (7.6 x 17.8 cm)

Thread in coordinating color

Tulle strips (2): 6 x 30 inches (15.2 x 76.2 cm)

3-D elements: assorted

Eyelet clamping tool

Eyelets (6)

Ribbon: 40 inches (101.6 cm)

1 Sew Base Fabric to Batting

Cut base fabric to measure 3 x 7 inches (7.6 x 17.8 cm). Place this onto a piece of batting and trim the batting so that it is slightly larger than the base on all sides. Sew all sides with a ¼-inch (.6 cm) seam allowance with a sewing machine. Add quilting stitches as desired.

2 Add the Tulle Edging

Fold each 6 x 30-inch (14.2 x 76.2 cm) tulle strip in half lengthwise. Gather and stitch the tulle along one edge to create pleats. Sew this edging to the long edges of the prepared base fabric and batting panel.

4 Line the Underside

Sew lining fabric to the underside of the cuff to cover the hand stitching. Add a label or other signature embellishment to the underside of the cuff as well.

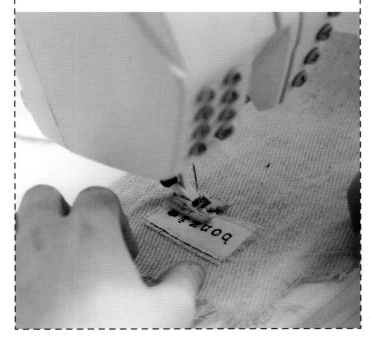

3 Add 3-D Elements

Use a hand needle and thread to stitch assorted 3-D elements to the cuff, including chains, buttons, and beading. Allow some elements to hang or dangle.

5 Add the Eyelets

Using a clamping tool, attach corset eyelets on both sides of the cuff. These eyelets will allow ribbon or cording to be laced through and tied to secure the cuff to the wearer's wrist.

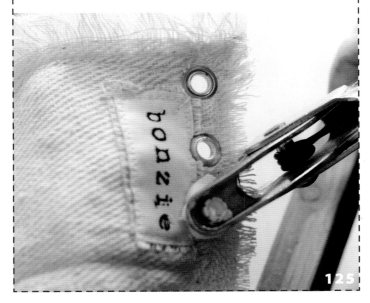

TEVA DURHAM

Teva Durham is a designer of knitted and crocheted wearable art who has created countless unique pieces and patterns. She founded one of the first online knitting design sites, and wrote *Loop-d-Loop: More than 40 Novel Designs for Knitters; Loop-d-Loop Crochet*; and *Loop-d-Lace*. Teva has also developed a line of yarns through www.tahkistacycharles.com, for which she produces designs twice a year. The minimalist yet romantic flair she often uses in her creations floods over into her personal style, which is exemplified in both her wardrobe and her home.

STYLISH INFLUENCES FROM NEW YORK TO PARIS

Teva has been interested in textiles and clothing from a very young age. "As a kid I remember being fascinated by the print of my mom's Marrimeko skirts," says Teva. "I used to draw paper dolls, make full pages of colorful, drawn fabric, and then cut and glue the dresses from them." And she definitely yearned for unique wardrobe items—at the age of eight she even convinced her parents to let her have a local shoemaker make her gladiator sandals from her own design.

Her curiosity grew when she moved from the Midwest to Manhattan to attend the High School of Performing Arts. "We had to come up with our own costumes for scene study," says Teva. "I began my love of scouring thrift shops and had quite the vintage dress and sweater collection. I loved to put together outfits that were like Madonna in *Desperately Seeking Susan*." When Teva was short on money, she would sell her one-of-a-kind artwear designs on the streets of New York.

In her early twenties, Teva worked in some SoHo boutiques, including the original Morgane Le Fay. "The energy of New York was an influence," says Teva of her emerging style, "and I also traveled to London, Paris, and Morocco searching for the glamorous kind of expat life." Teva still enjoys window-shopping on the streets of SoHo. As she has gotten older and become a mom, her style has become more down-to-earth and utilitarian. "But I have a vibrant, stylish alter ego in terms of who I design sweaters for," she says.

127

THE ESSENCE OF TEVA'S STYLE

- High-quality fabrics: "One thing I've learned is that cheap fabric doesn't feel good or look good. I love natural fibers, and often a high-end blend with a performance fiber, such as Lycra."

- Tunics worn over leggings or jeans with boots

- A great fitted jacket: "It's timeless, versatile, and worth every dollar."

- Parachute skirts: "These are a hip alternative to the peasant skirt."

- Boots, particularly square-toed ankle boots with a heel that is two or three inches high: they emphasize her long legs.

- Ballet flats, another favorite go-to item for Teva

1 Many of Teva's designs are edgy and romantic—they range from this belt to sweaters to tunics. **2** Part of Teva's creative process involves knitting swatches to experiment with design motifs. **3** Teva takes pride in using quality materials in all of her designs.

INTERESTING MINIMALISM

Teva is currently restoring a Victorian townhouse in a transitional, up-and-coming Jersey City neighborhood. She loves the French doors, grilled radiators, and curved wall of her studio, which she's painted a mauve color. "With all the construction and refinishing that comes with remodeling, I haven't completed the decorating yet," says Teva. "But I have started to assemble some pieces, and to make choices to express my attitude, and to make my studio function better for design work."

Her home reflects the style that is also evident in her personal wardrobe and her knitted works. "My knit and crochet designs are often architectural and minimalist, but with a romantic feel," says Teva. In addition to neutral tones with shots of intense painterly colors, Teva likes folkloric and nautical combinations, like white with blue or white with red: "I like a certain minimalism and interesting material—dark wood, glass, and brass, for example." The colors in a painting by her mother also inspired a few of her picks for her home.

128

MEETING DEADLINES & CONNECTING WITH ARTISTS

Teva's work keeps her busy. Knitting and writing knitting patterns are labor intensive, and she has frequent deadlines. She sends some work to sample knitters, but much of the time she sacrifices sleep and does the projects herself. "Luckily I have never lost my joy of the actual knitting," says Teva. "I love the meditative feeling of hours of repetitive motion. And the relief when the deadline is met makes me feel like I've run a marathon."

Teva often wakes up early to take advantage of those quiet hours before she has to get her daughter, Olivia, up for school. The rest of her morning consists of grinding her own coffee beans and popping in a load of laundry. Once Olivia is off to school, Teva spends the day working and meeting with other artists in the area. "I am fortunate to have found other creative spirits, especially single mothers with whom I share a special bond," says Teva. Most days, though, Teva has to hunker down with a calculator, graph paper, and computer to grade patterns for several hours. She'll often take a work-in-progress knitting project with her when she accompanies Olivia to after-school activities.

With all that's going on in Teva's life, she says one of the challenges she has is not lacking inspiration, but being overwhelmed with too many ideas that she doesn't know where to start. With the fabulous work she is known for, and the minimalist and romantic style she exudes, there is no question that those numerous ideas are translated with precision and beauty.

Teva has a special place in her heart for birds, partly because she grew up with a parrot, and she adores any decorative items that have birds on them. The wooden goose shown here was a gift from her mother.

SENSATIONAL STOCKINETTE BELT

This belt taps into Teva's **love** of **yarn**. It's a great project for stash yarn because a **thin panel** knitted in stockinette stitch is all that's needed. For this project, yarn from Teva's Loop-d-Loop line in the color Quartz was used.

WHAT YOU'LL NEED

DK-weight yarn:
(enough to knit the belt to fit desired waist)

Knitting needles: size 7 (4.5 cm)

Tulle: ¼ yard (22.9 cm)

Scissors

Rayon ribbon: 4 yards (365.8 cm) each in light gray and dark blue

Hand needle

Thread in coordinating color

Hook-and-eyes (4)

Metal ring

light
(3)
DK, Light, Worsted

1 Knit a Panel in Stockinette Stitch

Select a yarn and knit a gauge to determine how many stitches you will need to cast on to create a belt with the width you desire. After you cast on, knit the piece in stockinette stitch to a length that is suited for your waist. Bind off. Cut a piece of tulle the same size as the knit belt, place it onto the back of belt, and then pin the light gray rayon ribbon along the sides.

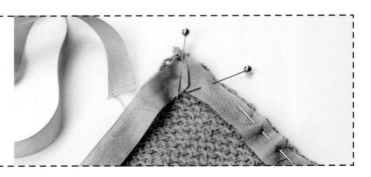

2 Stitch the Ribbon

With needle and thread, hand stitch the rayon ribbon to the tulle and belt.

3 Attach the Metal Ring

With a larger needle and the same yarn used for the knitted belt, position the metal ring on one end of the belt and hand stitch in place.

4 Stitch Small Fasteners

On the other end of the belt, use a needle and thread to stitch on the four eyes from the hook-and-eye fasteners.

5 Thread the Ribbon

Thread dark blue rayon ribbon through the eyes and through the metal ring with a nice crisscross effect.

6 Adjust as Desired

Depending on your outfit, adjust the dark blue ribbon to fit the belt looser or tighter as desired.

AMY TANGERINE

www.amytangerine.com
www.amytangerine.blogspot.com

What began as a fun way to embellish a T-shirt has grown into a company, and a name you won't forget—**Amy Tangerine**. Amy's reverse appliqué technique can now be seen on women's and children's wear in hundreds of boutiques across the world and online. Whether she's sporting a casual dress or one of her own handmade creations, she's a true example that being comfortable in your own skin is a style of its own.

A LIFE IN T-SHIRTS

When Amy first began her wearable line, she cut up old men's T-shirts into women's silhouettes. She was able to recycle shirts that couldn't be sold (because of holes in the sleeves or marks on the shirts) into great canvases for her art, and then she was able to use the scraps as embellishments as well. Since those early days, her line has grown tremendously. "In 2006, when we were shipping out shirts to over 200 stores, including Bloomingdale's and a number of international stores, I was nuts," shares Amy. From the moment she woke up to the time she went to bed, Amy worked. She traveled to trade shows and spent time managing the people who worked with her—she often ate lunch standing up or in front of the computer.

Amy was still able to produce about 15 new designs most months that year, even though she estimates that only ten percent of her time was spent creating. Amy's company shipped more than 30,000 women's and baby T-shirts during that time. In addition, she made personal appearances, collaborated with a friend on a book, and thought about growing her business. She looks back on the years between 2004 and 2007 as a blur. "I think of those as really great years for business, and not necessarily the best years of truly living," admits Amy. "I am going for more of a balance nowadays," she says, as she makes sure to include time to create for her own enjoyment.

1

2

3

❶ Amy's sofa is named Tangerina because Amy feels like it was made for her—she created the pillows herself to match. **❷** Vintage suitcases in funky colors provide added color and storage for Amy—and are added visual elements of her style in her home. **❸** A great jacket should be the final touch for today's business-casual look, says Amy. **❹** Using a roller skate as a bookend is an inventive way to add color and style to a shelf. **❺** Amykathryn purses are Amy's favorite with their color and pattern combinations.

4

5

THE ESSENCE OF AMY'S STYLE

- Comfort and confidence
- Minimal accessories
- One key statement piece per outfit
- Layering: "A T-shirt, jeans, nice shoes, and a blazer should be considered business-casual these days."

Shown here is a classic Amy look, with one of her T-shirts, a favorite pair of jeans, and her beloved cowboy boots. Here she's outside in her city of Venice, California, where she often takes walks to gather inspiration.

AMY'S PRIZED WEARABLES

- Dress from Thailand that Amy purchased in four different colors: She wishes she had bought 12 because they're so comfortable and versatile.
- Cowboy boots and Uggs: They've been such a staple in Amy's wardrobe for so many years that she doesn't know what she would wear without them.
- Fred Segal boots: "All at once amazing and the most money I have ever spent on a pair of shoes."
- Rebe hoodies
- Robin's Jeans
- Amykathryn purses: Amy receives so many compliments when she wears these colorful creations, and she admits to maybe owning a few too many.

IT'S THE LITTLE THINGS

In 2007, Amy discovered scrapbooking, which she enjoys immensely. Sometimes, when she's in need of inspiration, she'll turn to scrapbooking to get past a creative block. "I'll create scrapbook pages just for the heck of it," says Amy. "I may not even finish it, but as long as I snap out of the mood I was in before, it's fine." Along with scrapbooking, it's the little things in life that inspire Amy—a cute card, a simple act of kindness among strangers, good energy from good people, and design blogs. "And sometimes, if I'm still feeling uninspired, I'll just go and eat something," says Amy. "That always helps."

Amy enjoys mixing bits of color and pattern in her home to create an environment that invites inspiration. She loves her collection of books which are always patiently waiting for someone to pick up. "I also love my sofa, named Tangerina, because it looks like it was made for my place and me."

135

A TRANSFORMATIVE STYLE

Amy's mom and dad have been a huge influence on her. "They're both the most dedicated workers I know," says Amy. Her dad's rational, supportive, positive, and encouraging nature has inspired her to seek happiness always. Her mom is creative, and learned to make things out of necessity. Amy admires her strength and drive to succeed. "And, on a style note, my mom has passed along some of her fabulous wardrobe pieces from India (where both my parents were born and raised) to me." In fact, she says her mom has some serious style. "Back in the day, she definitely was at the forefront of all the trends," says Amy. "Looking at her old photos makes me wish she hadn't gotten rid of most of her wardrobe." Not only did her mom have some great pieces, she learned to sew so she could create the exact dress she wanted when she didn't have the money to spend.

Sometimes the outfits Amy wore growing up were not always the most stylish. "I lived through the '80s!" admits Amy. When she was young and trying to find her own style, Amy tried different looks according to what was trendy. She was interested in fashion, but didn't have the money to spend on it. "Making do with what you have can sometimes be good," shares Amy, "but it can also turn into what you see years down the road as a total disaster." Through her adolescent years, Amy stuck to basics with a little bit of a twist.

During college, she studied fashion and worked as a stylist. She credits those years as her transformative-style years. "I learned to stay on trend, but not go too crazy with the fads that passed very quickly. It helped to put models into clothing that I coveted. If a model didn't look good in it, there was no way I was pulling it off, so I didn't even have to try."

These days, whether it's riding her pink bike on the beach, taking her dogs for a walk, or designing the next fun color combination for her T-shirts, Amy tries to put a little twist on everything she wears—and a little twist on everything she does.

TIPS TO ENHANCE STYLE

- Confidence is key: "You can pull off even the quirkiest of pieces if you do it with confidence."

- Find something that you love to wear, so it can be your go-to outfit when you're looking for something comfortable and stylish.

- Expand and experiment with a formula that you know works for you.

- Invest in great dresses because they're simple—you only have to think about one item.

- Look for fun accessories, which can add an interesting element to an already stylish outfit.

1 Amy loves her collection of books just waiting in stacks to be picked up and read. 2 Amy always tries to put a little twist on what she wears, and adding hair accessories, like this handmade one, is one of her favorite ways to do that. 3 Pops of color against a darker neutral color is a favorite color palette. 4 Uggs have been a staple in her wardrobe for years. 5 Amy often travels the streets of Venice Beach in her trusty roller skates.

137

Amy started creating reverse appliqué T-shirts years ago when she wanted to find a crafty way to **embellish a shirt**. She thought it seemed so much **cooler** to put the **fabric behind the shirt** as opposed to simply on top.

WHAT YOU'LL NEED

T-shirt

Paper (optional for template)

Ballpoint pen

Floral fabric cotton panel: 6 x 14 inches (15.2 x 35.6 cm)

Hand needle

Embroidery floss

CRAFTY APPLIQUÉ T-SHIRT

1 Trace a Template

Find a plain T-shirt. Draw the design either on a template or directly on the front of the shirt with a ballpoint pen (if you're planning on making more than one, it's worth it to make a template).

2 Find a Contrasting Fabric

Find a contrasting fabric and cut out a piece, making sure it's large enough to cover the design. Pin the fabric to the inside of the shirt under your design.

3 Sew the Fabric

Using embroidery floss, start sewing ¼ inch (.6 cm) outside the pen line, and continue around the entire design. Make sure the knots are secure. (If you're sewing letters down, knot and finish off each letter rather than leaving too big of a stitch in between the letters.)

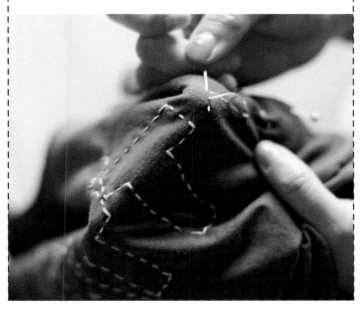

4 Cut Around the Back Fabric

After the entire design is sewn, turn the shirt inside out. Carefully cut ½ inch (1.3 cm) around the fabric.

5 Cut Out the Front Fabric

Turn the shirt right side out and begin carefully cutting on the line. Be sure you're only cutting the T-shirt fabric. Cut out each piece to reveal all your hard work.

PROJECT TEMPLATES

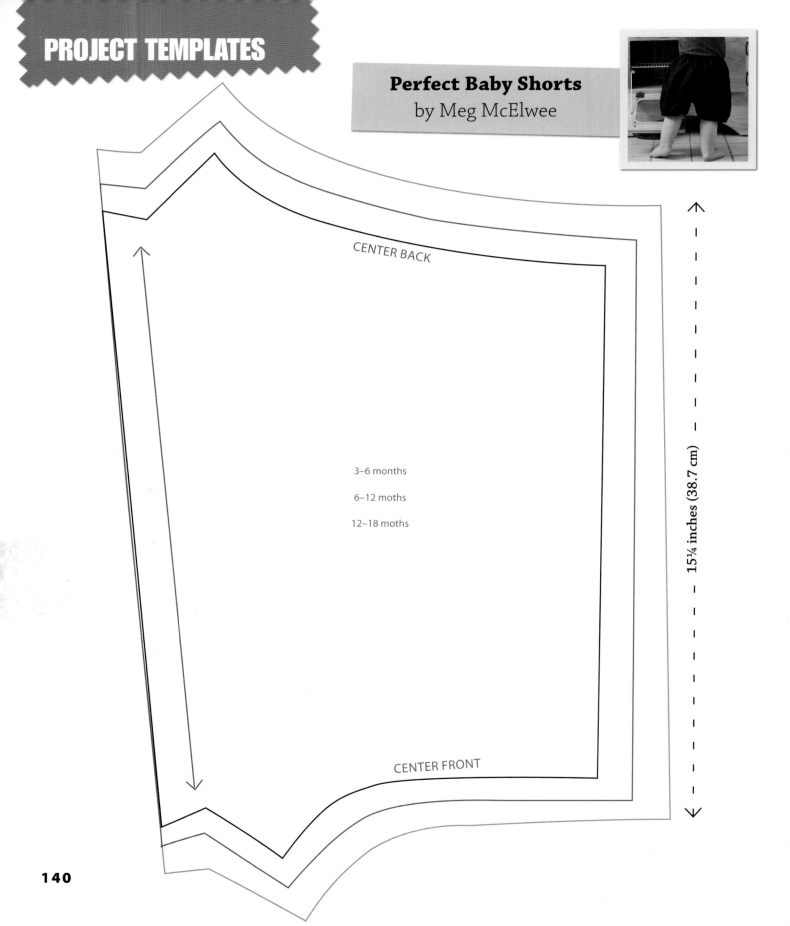

CENTER BACK

3–6 months

6–12 moths

12–18 moths

15¼ inches (38.7 cm)

CENTER FRONT

140

Chunky & Leafy Felt Headband
by Elsie Flannigan

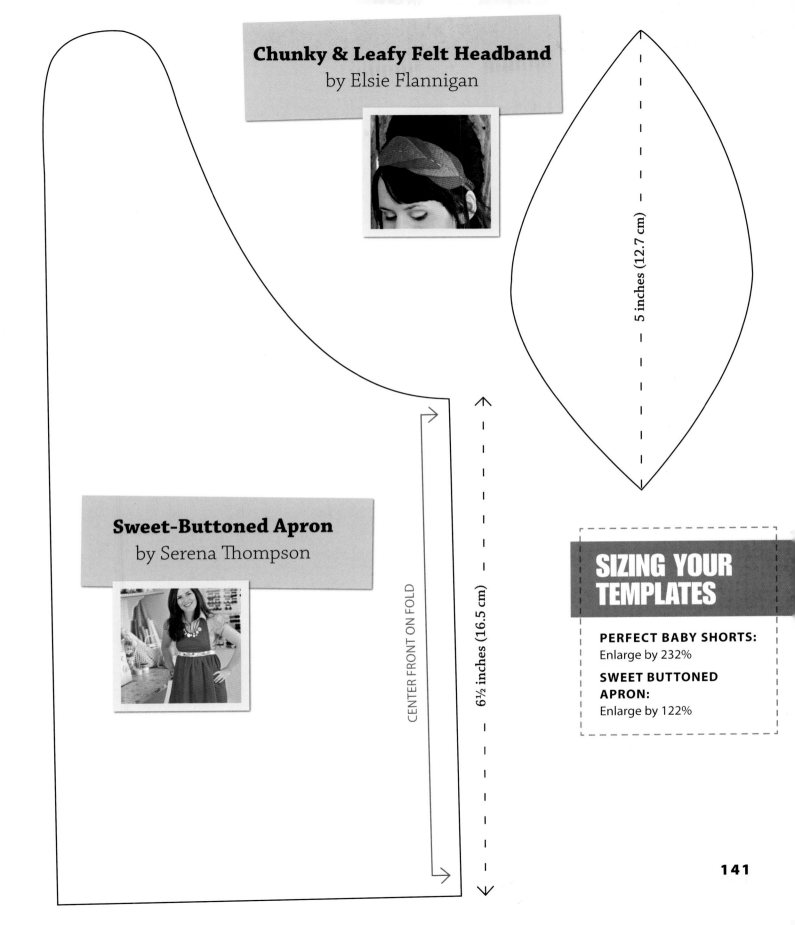

5 inches (12.7 cm)

Sweet-Buttoned Apron
by Serena Thompson

CENTER FRONT ON FOLD

6½ inches (16.5 cm)

SIZING YOUR TEMPLATES

PERFECT BABY SHORTS:
Enlarge by 232%

SWEET BUTTONED APRON:
Enlarge by 122%

141

PROJECT TEMPLATES

**Rockin'
Retro Capelet**
by Meg Allan Cole

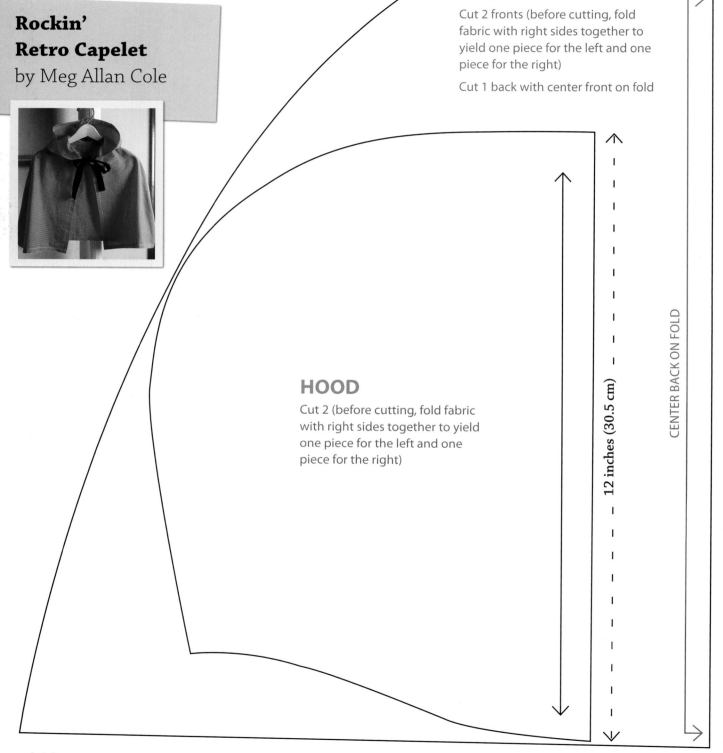

BODY

Cut 2 fronts (before cutting, fold fabric with right sides together to yield one piece for the left and one piece for the right)

Cut 1 back with center front on fold

HOOD

Cut 2 (before cutting, fold fabric with right sides together to yield one piece for the left and one piece for the right)

12 inches (30.5 cm)

CENTER BACK ON FOLD

16 inches (40.6 cm)

Pretty Patchwork Tote
by Rashida Coleman-Hale

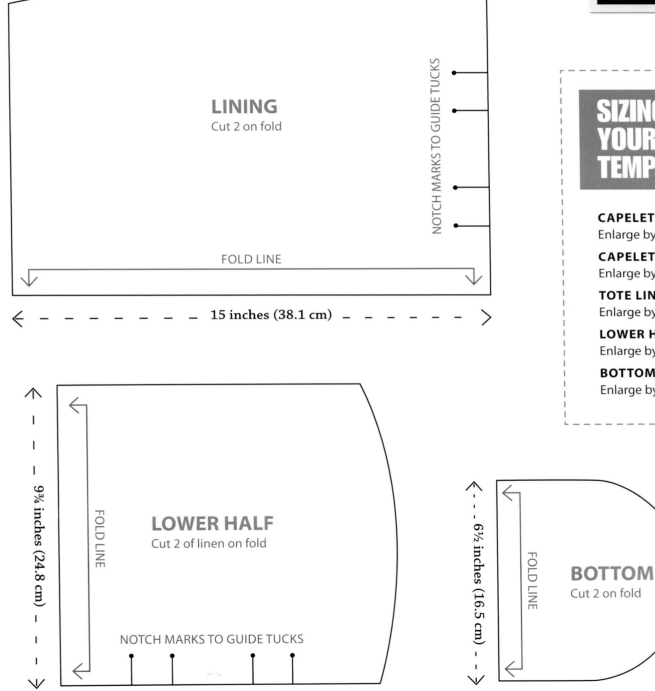

LINING
Cut 2 on fold

NOTCH MARKS TO GUIDE TUCKS

FOLD LINE

← — — — — — — 15 inches (38.1 cm) — — — — — — →

LOWER HALF
Cut 2 of linen on fold

FOLD LINE

9¾ inches (24.8 cm)

NOTCH MARKS TO GUIDE TUCKS

SIZING YOUR TEMPLATES

CAPELET BODY:
Enlarge by 194%

CAPELET HOOD:
Enlarge by 184%

TOTE LINING:
Enlarge by 300%

LOWER HALF:
Enlarge by 300%

BOTTOM:
Enlarge by 300%

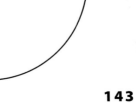

BOTTOM
Cut 2 on fold

FOLD LINE

6½ inches (16.5 cm)

143

YARN WEIGHT CHART

YARN WEIGHT SYMBOL + CATEGORIES	lace (0)	super fine (1)	fine (2)	light (3)	medium (4)	bulky (5)	super bulky (6)
TYPE OF YARNS IN CATEGORY	Fingering, 10-count crochet thread	Sock, Fingering, Baby	Sport, Baby	DK, Light, Worsted	Worsted, Afghan, Aran	Chunky, Craft, Rug	Bulky, Roving

Source: Craft Yarn Council of America's www.yarnstandards.com

144